# HAMILTON BEACH TOASTER OVEN COOKBOOK

---

90 FOOLPROOF RECIPES FOR QUICKER,
HEALTHIER AND MORE DELICIOUS MEALS
THAT ANYONE CAN COOK.

ALICIA MILLNER

# CONTENTS

*Introduction*      ix

## BREAKFASTS RECIPES

1. Savory Monkey Bread      3
2. Bacon and Egg Toast cups      5
3. Shakshuka Avocado      7
4. Hamilton Beach' Toaster Oven Baked Eggs with Green Beans      9
5. Hamilton Beach' Toaster Baked Oatmeal      11
6. Vegetable Breakfast Casserole      13
7. Greek Frittata      15
8. Baked French Toast      17
9. Hamilton Beach' Toaster Oven Egg Bake      19
10. Bacon, Egg, and Cheese Breakfast Hash      21

## DESSERT AND SNACK RECIPES

11. Spinach Beef Pie      25
12. Ole Polenta Casserole      27
13. Ham and veggie Casserole      29
14. Hamilton Beach' Toaster Oven Kale Chips      31
15. Zucchini Hamburger Pie      33
16. Pepperoni Roll-ups      35
17. Two-potato Shepherd's Pie      37
18. Spaghetti Pie      39
19. Butternut Squash Mac and Cheese      41
20. Asparagus and Ham Strata      43

## BEEF RECIPES

21. Hamilton Beach" Toaster Oven Meatloaf   47
22. Hamilton Beach' Toaster Oven Broiled Flank Steak   49
with Herb Oil
23. Hamilton Beach' Toaster Oven Italian Hot Dish   51
24. Mozzarella Baked Spaghetti   53
25. Bake once, Eat twice Lasanga   55
26. Spaghetti Casserole Bake   57
27. Lasagna Rolls   59
28. Chipotle Mac and Cheese   61
29. Vegetable and Beef Stuffed Red Peppers   63
30. Salt and Pepper Beef Roast   65

# PORK RECIPES

31. Hamilton Beach' Toaster Oven Broiled Pork Chops   69
32. Hamilton Beach' Toaster Oven Pork Loin   71
33. Cajun Pork Chops   73
34. Pork Tenderloin with Carrots   75
35. Pork Belly and Red Cabbage   77
36. Broiled Pork Chops with Hot Cherry Pepper   79
37. Baked Pork Chops   81
38. Broiled Boneless Pork Chops   83
39. Baked Boneless Pork Chops   85
40. Golden Baked pork Cutlets   87

# LAMB RECIPES

41. Herb Toasted Lamb Chops   91
42. Classic Rack of Lamb in the Hamilton Beach'   93
Toaster Oven
43. Toasted Rack of Lamb   95
44. Broiled Rosemary Lamb Chops   97
45. Leg of Lamb   99
46. Lamb with Rosemary and Garlic   101
47. Lamb Loin Chops   103
48. Hamilton Beach' Toaster Oven Lamb Chops   105
49. Baked Lamb Chops   107
50. Roast Lamb with Rosemary and Garlic   109

# CHICKEN AND TURKEY RECIPES

51. BBQ and Ranch Chicken Pizza     113
52. Chicken Tater Bake     115
53. Chicken Club Pizza     117
54. Chicken Tater Tot Casserole     119
55. Turkey Mushroom Tetrazzini     121
56. Chicken Cordon Bleu Bake     123
57. Chicken Club Casseroles     125
58. Golden Chicken Cordon Bleu     127
59. Turkey Meatloaf     129
60. Chicken Reuben Roll-ups     131

# FISH AND SEAFOOD RECIPES

61. Shrimp with Garlic Butter     135
62. Hamilton Beach' Toaster Oven Salmon     137
63. Hamilton Beach' Toaster Oven Baked Sole with Asparagus     139
64. Garlic Butter Orange Roughly     141
65. Salmon and Asparagus     143
66. Hamilton Beach' Toaster Oven Salt Grilled Mackerel     145
67. Walnut and Oat-crusted Salmon     147
68. Walnut-crusted Ginger salmon     149
69. Hamilton Beach' Toaster Oven Baked Shrimp     151
70. Cheesy Baked Salmon     153

# BREAD, BAGEL, AND PIZZA RECIPES

71. Hamilton Beach' Toaster Oven Banana Bread     157
72. Hamilton Beach' Toaster Oven Baguettes     159
73. Pumpkin Bread     161
74. Hamilton Beach' Toaster Oven Bagel Chips     163
75. Hamilton Beach' Toaster Oven Fruit Pizzas     165
76. English Muffin Pizza     167
77. Pizza Toast     169

78. Hamilton Beach' Toaster Oven Pizza Bagels     171
79. Hamilton Beach' Toaster Oven Sandwiches     173
80. Mini Bagel Pizza Snacks     175

## VEGAN AND VEGETARIAN RECIPES

81. Hamilton Beach' Toaster Oven Veggie Nachos     179
82. Hamilton Beach' Toaster Oven Baked Tofu     181
83. Garlicky Mushrooms     183
84. Toaster Oven vegetables     185
85. Hamilton Beach' Toaster Oven Brussels Sprouts     187
86. Green Bean Casserole     189
87. Vegan Green Beans Casserole     191
88. Yogurt Cornbread     193
89. Lentil Loaf     195
90. Scalloped Potatoes     197

*Conclusion*     199

# INTRODUCTION

You won't find a design like the Hamilton Beach Easy Reach Toaster Oven with Roll-Top Door anywhere else. Its unique and large opening make food easy to reach.

And since the door opens above the oven, it frees up your countertop space in front. Best of all, it's easy to keep clean because food can't spill on the door.

With a 6 slice toast capacity and four cooking settings, you can enjoy everything from crispy toast, broiled fish and mouth-watering roasted vegetables. Easy dials make it simple to choose bake, broil and toast settings.

This oven also has convection technology using a top and bottom heating element and a built-in fan to distribute heat evenly for a uniform temperature. It also features a 30 minute timer with auto shutoff, so you know when your food is ready. Or you can choose an optional stay-on setting for food requiring more time. The Easy Reach Toaster Oven comes with a bake pan, bake rack and removable crumb tray.

# BREAKFASTS RECIPES

# 1

## SAVORY MONKEY BREAD

**Preparation Time :** 10 minutes

**Cooking Time :** 45 minutes

**Serving :** 4

**Ingredients :**

•3 slices of bacon

•¼ stick butter

•¾ biscuit dough tube

•1 egg

•1 tbsp milk

•¾ cup cheese, shredded

**Preparation :**

1.Set the temperature knob of the Hamilton Beach' toaster oven to bake setting.

2.Rotate the timer knob (med) and let the toaster oven preheat to 400°F.

3.Place bacon on the pan and cook for 20 minutes.

4.Dice the cooked bacon into bite-size pieces

5.Fold a double layer of tin foil around a box to make a container for the bread.

6.Put butter in the tin foil and melt it in the toaster oven on low heat.

7.Form balls with the dough and place them in the tin foil. Add egg, milk, cheese, and cooked bacon to the container and mix well.

8.Rotate the timer knob to reduce the heat to 350°F.

9.Place the tin foil on the tray at the bottom position and bake for 25 minutes or until golden brown.

10. Serve and enjoy.

Serving suggestions : serve with a hot cup of coffee.

Variation tip : use your favourite type of cheese

**Nutritional value per Serving :** Calories: 440 kcal, Protein: 5g, Fat: 20g, Carbs: 61g

# BACON AND EGG TOAST CUPS

**Preparation Time :** 10 minutes
**Cooking Time :** 20 minutes
**Serving :** 4
**Ingredients :**
•4 strips of bacon
•2 slices of bread
•4 eggs
•Salt and pepper
**Preparation :**
1.Cook bacon on a skillet for 3 minutes or until almost crispy. Set aside to let cool.

2.Meanwhile, oil a muffin tin and set the temperature knob of the Hamilton Beach' toaster oven to bake setting.

3.Rotate the timer knob (Dark) and let the toaster oven preheat to 350°F.

4.Remove crust from bread slices, half them, and press each on the muffin tray.

5.Place the cooked bacon on the bread in a circular shape then crack an egg on each tin.

6.Season with salt and pepper to taste.

7.Place the muffin tin on the toaster oven tray at the bottom position and bake for 20 minutes or until the egg is set.

8.Serve.

Serving suggestions : serve garnished with green onions and chives with a cup of coffee

Variation tip : Season with everything bagel seasonings

**Nutritional value per Serving :** Calories: 217kcal, Protein: 12g, Fat: 12g, Carbs: 16g

# 3

## SHAKSHUKA AVOCADO

Preparation Time: 5 minutes
   Cooking Time: 20 minutes
   Serving: 1
   Ingredients:
   •$\frac{1}{2}$ avocado
   •1 egg
   •1 tbsp marinara sauce
   •$\frac{1}{2}$ basil leaf
   •1 tbsp feta cheese
   Preparation:
   1.Slice the avocado into half and scoop out the pit and some avocado.
   2.Crack an egg in the avocado then form a bowl around the avocado using a tin foil.
   3.Set the temperature knob of the Hamilton Beach' toaster oven to bake setting F.
   4.Rotate the timer knob (Med) and let the toaster oven preheat to 425°
   5.Place the tin foil on the tray at the bottom position and cook for 15 minutes

Serving suggestions: serve with sauce, basil leaf, and cheese

Variation tip: you can replace the marinara sauce with tomato sauce

Nutritional value per serving: Calories: 210 kcal, Protein: 11g, Fat: 12g, Carbs: 14g

# HAMILTON BEACH' TOASTER OVEN BAKED EGGS WITH GREEN BEANS

**Preparation Time :** 8 minutes
**Cooking Time :** 12 minutes
**Serving :** 2
**Ingredients :**
•8 oz green beans, fresh and ends trimmed
•½ tbsp grapeseed oil
•2 eggs
•2 tbsp half and half
•4 tbsp parmesan cheese
•Salt and pepper to taste
•2 slices bread
**Preparation :**
1.Adjust the rack to the bottom position then set the temperature knob of the Hamilton Beach' toaster oven to bake setting F.

2.Rotate the timer knob (light) and let the toaster oven preheat to 425°

3.Meanwhile, combine the green beans with oil on the baking sheet then season them with salt and pepper.

4.Add 2 lightly greased ramekins on the baking sheet. Crack an egg on each ramekin and season it with salt and pepper.

5.Place the baking sheet on the rack in the toaster oven and cook for 6 minutes.

6.Remove the baking sheet from the toaster oven and stir the beans. Place bread slices at the edge of the sheet.

7.Continue to cook for an additional 7 minutes. Serve and enjoy.

Serving suggestions : Serve with fresh basil, parsley, or your favourite herbs

Variation tip : Use olive oil in place of grapeseed oil

**Nutritional value per Serving :** Calories: 259kcal, Protein: 16g, Fat: 11g, Carbs: 25g

# HAMILTON BEACH' TOASTER BAKED OATMEAL

**Preparation Time :** 15 minutes
**Cooking Time :** 30 minutes
**Serving :** 2
**Ingredients :**
• 1 ripe banana, mashed
• 1 tbsp Flax meal
• 2 tbsp pure Maple Syrup
• 2 tbsp olive oil
• ½ tbsp cinnamon, round
• ½ tbsp vanilla extract
• ¼ tbsp baking powder
• ⅛ tbsp sea salt
• ½ cup almond milk
• 1 cup rolled oats
• ¼ cup pecan pieces

**Preparation :**

1.Adjust the rack to the bottom position then set the temperature knob of the Hamilton Beach' toaster oven to bake setting F.

2.Rotate the timer knob( Dark) and let the toaster oven preheat to 350°F

3.Grease a baking dish with oil.

4.In a mixing bowl, add banana and mash well. Stir in flax meal, maple syrup, oil, cinnamon, vanilla, baking powder, sea salt, almond milk, oats, and pecans.

5.Pour the mixture into the baking dish and place the dish on the rack.

6.Bake for 25 minutes or until the oatmeal is set and browned on the edges.

7.Let the oatmeal sit for 10 minutes before serving. Enjoy.

Serving suggestions : Serve the oatmeal with banana slices

Variation tip : use soy milk in place of almond milk

**Nutritional value per Serving :** Calories: 235 kcal, Protein: 5g, Fat: 13g, Carbs: 29g

## 6

---

# VEGETABLE BREAKFAST CASSEROLE

**Preparation Time :** 20 minutes
**Cooking Time :** 60 minutes
**Serving :** 5
**Ingredients :**
• 1 tbsp olive oil
• 3 Yukon potatoes
• ¼ cup minced onion
• 2 cups chopped veggies such as asparagus, zucchini, mushrooms, tomatoes, and spinach
• ¾ cup cheddar cheese, grated
• 8 eggs
• 1 ½ tsp milk
• ½ tbsp garlic powder

**Preparation :**
1.Adjust the rack to the bottom position then set the temperature knob of the Hamilton Beach" toaster oven to bake setting F.

2.Rotate the timer knob( Med) and let the toaster oven preheat to 350°F.

3.Meanwhile, heat ½ tbsp of olive oil on a pan over medium heat.

4.Add potatoes and cook for 5 minutes or until they start to brown. Stir in onions and continue to cook for 5 minutes.

5.Transfer from the pan to the casserole dish.

6.Add the vegetables to the pan and cook for 3 minutes or until they start to soften.

7.Add the vegetables to the casserole dish and top with cheese.

8.Beat eggs in a bowl and add milk. Stir in garlic powder. Pour the mixture over the vegetables in the casserole dish

9.Rotate the timer knob to the Stay-on setting and bake for 45 minutes or until the egg is well cooked. Serve and enjoy.

Serving suggestions : Serve with a hot cup of coffee

Variation tip : Add sausage or bacon to the casserole for a meaty breakfast

**Nutritional value per Serving :** Calories: 268 kcal, Protein: 16g, Fat: 19g, Carbs: 9g

# 7

# GREEK FRITTATA

**Preparation Time :** 10 minutes
**Cooking Time :** 25 minutes
**Serving :** 4
**Ingredients :**
•3 tbsp olive oil
•10 eggs
•2 tbsp kosher salt
•½ tbsp black pepper
•5 oz baby spinach
•10 oz grape tomatoes, halved
•4 thinly sliced scallions
•8 oz crumbled feta
**Preparation :**
1.Set the temperature knob of the Hamilton Beach' toaster oven to bake setting.
2.Set the timer knob to light and allow the toaster oven to preheat to 350°F.
3.Pour the oil into a casserole dish and place it in the toaster oven rack. Close the door.
4.Heat the casserole dish for 5 minutes.

5.Meanwhile, whisk the eggs, salt, and pepper in a mixing bowl.

6.Stir in the spinach, tomatoes, and scallions to the egg mixture until they are well combined.

7.Add the feta to the mixture and gently stir until well mixed.

8.When the timer has gone off remove the casserole from the oven and pour the mixture.

9.Set the timer to bake the frittata for 25 minutes.

10. Transfer the frittata to a serving platter.

11. Serve and enjoy.

Serving suggestions : serve this frittata with sautéed greens, or salami.

Variation tip : feta cheese can be replaced with parmesan cheese.

**Nutritional value per Serving :** Calories: 461 kcal, Protein: 26g, Fat: 35g, Carbs: 8g

# 8

# BAKED FRENCH TOAST

**Preparation Time :** 5 minutes
  **Cooking Time :** 15 minutes
  **Serving :** 4
  **Ingredients :**
  •Cooking spray
  •1 egg
  •1 tbsp vanilla extract
  •1 tbsp brown sugar
  •¼ tbsp cinnamon, ground
  •Dash of salt
  •1 tbsp melted butter
  •½ cup milk
  •4 slices of quality sandwich bread
  **Preparation :**
  1.Set the temperature knob of the Hamilton Beach' toaster oven to bake setting.
  2.Set the timer knob to light and allow the toaster oven to preheat to 425° F.
  3.Spray a baking sheet with cooking spray.

4.In a bowl whisk the egg, vanilla, sugar, cinnamon, and salt until the sugar dissolves.

5.Whisk butter, and milk into the egg mixture.

6.Transfer the butter mixture to a shallow dish.

7.Coat both sides of the bread slices with the mixture.

8.Transfer the coated slices onto the baking sheet and bake the slices for 10 minutes.

9.When the timer has gone off, set the temperature knob of the toaster oven to the broil setting.

10. Set the timer to broil the slices for 5 minutes.

11. Transfer the French toast to a serving platter.

12. Serve and enjoy.

Serving suggestions : serve this French toast with fruit or syrup.

Variation tip : the quality sandwich bread can be replaced with Texas toast.

**Nutritional value per Serving :** Calories: 141 kcal, Protein: 5g, Fat: 6g, Carbs: 16g

**9**

---

# HAMILTON BEACH' TOASTER OVEN EGG BAKE

**Preparation Time :** 10 minutes
**Cooking Time :** 30 minutes
**Serving :** 2
**Ingredients :**
•Cooking spray
•3 eggs, beaten
•4 oz low fat cottage cheese
•2 oz pepper jack cheese, shredded
•½ jalapeno
•¼ cup canned corn, drained
•⅛ tbsp sea salt, fine
•Pinch of black pepper
**Preparation :**
1.Set the temperature knob of the Hamilton Beach' toaster oven to bake setting.
2.Rotate the timer knob to light and preheat the toaster oven to 350° F.
3.Spray the baking dish with cooking spray.
4.In a bowl mix the eggs, cottage cheese, pepper jack cheese,

jalapeno, corn, salt, and black pepper until they are well combined.

5.Pour the egg mixture on the baking dish and bake for 25 minutes.

6.Transfer the egg bake to a serving platter and allow it to cool.

7.Serve and enjoy.

Serving suggestions : serve this egg bake with toppings such as avocado, salsa, and fresh cilantro.

Variation tip : the jalapenos can be replaced with roasted broccoli.

**Nutritional value per Serving :** Calories: 201 kcal, Protein: 20g, Fat: 11g, Carbs: 7g

## 10

# BACON, EGG, AND CHEESE BREAKFAST HASH

**Preparation Time :** 5 minutes
   **Cooking Time :** 25 minutes
   **Serving :** 1
   **Ingredients :**
   •2 slices bacon
   •4 potatoes, diced
   •¼ tomato, diced
   •1 egg
   •¼ cup cheddar cheese, shredded
   **Preparation :**
   1.Set the temperature knob of the Hamilton Beach' toaster oven to bake setting.
   2.Rotate the timer knob to light and preheat the toaster oven to 350° F.
   3.Form a bowl using a double layer of tin foil.
   4.Place the bacon in the bowl and add the potatoes and tomato on top of the bacon.
   5.Crack the egg on top of the tomato.
   6.Place the bowl in the toaster oven rack and close the door.
   7.Bake the bacon hash for 20 minutes.

8.Remove the bacon hash from the toaster oven then add the cheese and allow it to melt.

9.Serve and enjoy.

Serving suggestions : serve this bacon hash with sautéed veggies.

Variation tip : cheddar cheese can be replaced with the favourite cheese.

**Nutritional value per Serving :** Calories: 1606 kcal, Protein: 54g, Fat: 41g, Carbs: 261g

# DESSERT AND SNACK
# RECIPES

# 11

---

# SPINACH BEEF PIE

**Preparation Time :** 25 minutes
**Cooking Time :** 30 minutes
**Serving :** 8
**Ingredients :**
• 1 cup all-purpose flour
• ⅓ cup oats
• 7 tbsp cold butter
• 3 tbsp cold water
• 1 lb ground beef
• 1 onion, chopped
• 1 green pepper, chopped
• 1 garlic clove, minced
• ¼ cup ketchup
• 1 tbsp salt
• 1 tbsp dried oregano
• ½ tbsp dried basil
• ½ tbsp marjoram dried
• ¼ tbsp pepper
• 10 oz spinach, chopped
• 3 eggs, beaten

•2 cups cheddar cheese

•1 tomato, seeded and diced

**Preparation :**

1.In a mixing bowl, mix flour, oats, and butter until crumbly. Add water gradually while tossing with a fork to form a ball.

2.Roll out the dough on a pie plate and trim the edges.

3.Cook beef, onions, green pepper, and garlic in a skillet over medium heat until the meat is no longer pink.

4.Stir in ketchup and seasonings then fold in spinach. let cool slightly.

5.stir in the egg and half the cheese until well mixed. Spoon the mixture into the crust.

6.Bake for 30 minutes at 400°F or until the center is set.

7.Sprinkle tomatoes and the remaining cheese around the edges. Bake for an additional 10 minutes or until the cheese has melted.

8.Let stand for 10 minutes

Serving suggestions : serve with freshly made juice

Variation tip : you can substitute green peppers with mushrooms

**Nutritional value per Serving :** Calories: 430 kcal, Protein:24 Fat: 27g, Carbs: 23g

# OLE POLENTA CASSEROLE

**Preparation Time :** 1 hour
**Cooking Time :** 45 minutes
**Serving :** 6
**Ingredients :**
- 1 cup yellow cornmeal
- 1 tbsp salt
- 4 cups water
- 1 lb ground beef
- 1 cup onions, chopped
- $\frac{1}{2}$ cup green pepper, chopped
- 2 garlic cloves, minced
- 14 $\frac{1}{2}$ oz tomatoes
- 8 oz tomato sauce
- $\frac{1}{2}$ lb fresh mushrooms, sliced
- 1 tbsp each dried basil, dill weed, and oregano
- Dash of hot sauce
- 1 $\frac{1}{2}$ cup mozzarella cheese, shredded
- $\frac{1}{4}$ cup parmesan cheese

**Preparation :**

1.In a mixing bowl, mix cornmeal, salt, and 1 cup of water until smooth.

2.Bring the remaining water to boil in a saucepan over medium heat. Add cornmeal mixture and bring to boil while stirring constantly.

3.Cook for 3 minutes until thickened. Reduce heat and simmer for 15 minutes. Divide the mixture between 2 greased baking dishes. Cover and refrigerate for 1 ½ hours or until firm.

4.Cook beef, onions, pepper, and garlic in a skillet over medium heat. Stir in tomatoes, tomato sauce, mushrooms, herbs, and hot sauce.

5.Bring the mixture to boil, then reduce heat and simmer for 20 minutes or until thickened.

6.Loosen 1 polenta from the sides of the baking dish and invert it lined baking sheet. Set aside.

7.Spoon half of the meat mixture over the other polenta. Sprinkle with half the cheeses.

8.Top with the reserved polenta and remaining meat mixture. cover and bake for 40 minutes at 350°F.

9.Uncover, sprinkle the remaining cheese and bake for an additional 10 minutes. Let sit before serving.

Serving suggestions : serve with sauce of choice

Variation tip : season the meat with granulated garlic

**Nutritional value per Serving :** Calories: 345 kcal, Protein: 25g, Fat: 14g, Carbs: 29g

## 13

# HAM AND VEGGIE CASSEROLE

**Preparation Time :** 10 minutes
**Cooking Time :** 20 minutes
**Serving :** 4
**Ingredients :**
•16 oz broccoli florets, cooked
•16 oz cauliflower, cooked
•4 tbsp butter
•¼ cup breadcrumbs, seasoned
•2 tbsp all-purpose flour
•1 ½ cups milk
•¾ cup cheddar cheese, shredded
•½ cup parmesan cheese, grated
•1 ½ cup fully cooked ham, cubed
•¼ tbsp pepper
**Preparation :**
1.Set the temperature knob of the Hamilton Beach' toaster oven to bake setting. Rotate the timer knob to allow the toaster oven to preheat to 425°F.
2.Meanwhile, melt 2 tbsp butter in a skillet. Add breadcrumbs and cook for 3 minutes or until toasted.

3.In a saucepan, melt the remaining butter over medium heat while stirring until smooth. Stir in flour and milk then bring to boil.

4.Cook for 2 minutes or until it thickens. Stir in cheese until well blended.

5.Stir in ham, and pepper. Transfer the mixture to a greased baking dish. Sprinkle toasted breadcrumbs.

6.Bake while uncovered for 15 minutes. Serve and enjoy.

Serving suggestions : serve with sautéed veggies of choice

Variation tip : you can use leftover ham in place of fresh ham. Any time of cheese available can be used.

**Nutritional value per Serving :** Calories: 420 kcal, Protein: 28g, Fat: 23g, Carbs: 25g

# 14

## HAMILTON BEACH' TOASTER OVEN KALE CHIPS

**Preparation Time :** 5 minutes
**Cooking Time :** 15 minutes
**Serving :** 1
**Ingredients :**
• 2 leaves kale
• 1 tbsp lemon peel
• Olive oil cooking spray
• Salt to taste
**Preparation :**
1. Set the temperature knob of the Hamilton Beach' toaster oven to bake setting.

2. Rotate the timer knob to allow the toaster oven to preheat to 425°F and place the rack at the bottom position.

3. Wash the kale leaves and pat them dry with paper towels. Tear the leaves into small equal pieces.

4. Arrange the leaves on a cookie sheet then spray 3 sprays of cooking spray.

5. Rub the kale around the cookie sheet to ensure that the bottom is well coated with oil.

6.Ensure the kale pieces don't overlap then sprinkle with salt and lemon zest.

7.Bake for 6 minutes, flip the pieces and bake for additional 5 minutes or until the leaves are crispy and dry.

8.Allow the chips to cool before serving. Enjoy.

Serving suggestions : serve with pasta or scrambled eggs

Variation tip : add seasonings such as garlic and fresh herbs of choice

**Nutritional value per Serving :** Calories: 70 kcal, Protein: 4g, Fat: 2g, Carbs: 9g

# ZUCCHINI HAMBURGER PIE

**Preparation Time :** 25 minutes
**Cooking Time :** 1 hour
**Serving :** 8
**Ingredients :**
•½ lb ground beef
•¼ cup onion, finely chopped
•1 tbsp salt
•½ tbsp garlic salt
•½ green pepper, diced
•1 tbsp dried oregano
•1 tbsp dried parsley flakes
•½ cup dry bread crumbs
•¼ cup parmesan cheese, grated
•1 egg, lightly beaten
•Pastry for double-crust pie
•4 cups zucchini, sliced
•2 tomatoes, thinly sliced
**Preparation :**
1.Brown the beef together with onions, salt, and garlic salt in a skillet.

2.Drain the beef and stir in green pepper, oregano, parsley, bread crumbs, cheese, and egg.

3.Put the pastry in the pie plate and layer 2 cups of zucchini.

4.Cover the pie crust with the beef mixture then top with tomatoes.

5.Layer the remaining zucchini and top with the pastry.

6.Set the temperature knob of the Hamilton Beach' toaster oven to bake setting.

7.Rotate the timer knob to light and allow the toaster oven to preheat to 350° F.

8.Cut a few slits on the top of the crust and transfer the pie into the toaster oven.

9.Set the timer to bake the pie for 1 hour.

10. Transfer the pie to a serving platter.

11. Serve and enjoy.

Serving suggestions : serve this zucchini pie with fruit salad.

Variation tip : green peppers can be replaced with celery.

**Nutritional value per Serving :** Calories: 353 kcal, Protein: 11g, Fat: 19g, Carbs: 36g

## 16

# PEPPERONI ROLL-UPS

**Preparation Time :** 10 minutes
   **Cooking Time :** 10 minutes
   **Serving :** 8
   **Ingredients :**
   •8 oz refrigerated crescent rolls
   •16 slices pepperoni, cut into quarters
   •2 string cheese, cut into quarters
   •$\frac{3}{4}$ tbsp Italian seasoning
   •$\frac{1}{4}$ tbsp garlic salt
   **Preparation :**
   1.Set the temperature knob of the Hamilton Beach' toaster oven to bake setting.
   2.Rotate the timer knob to med and allow the toaster oven to preheat to 375° F.
   3.Unroll the crescent rolls and place a pepperoni piece on each.
   4.Place a piece of cheese on the side of the dough and sprinkle it with $\frac{1}{2}$ tablespoon Italian seasoning.
   5.Roll the dough and pinch the end to seal.
   6.Sprinkle the rolls with garlic salt and remaining seasoning.

7.Place the rolls on a baking tray and bake them for 10 minutes.

8.Transfer the rolls to the serving platter.

9.Serve and enjoy.

Serving suggestions : serve these pepperoni rolls with salad.

Variation tip : string cheese can be replaced with pepper jack cheese.

**Nutritional value per Serving :** Calories: 282 kcal, Protein: 7g, Fat: 17g, Carbs: 22g

# TWO-POTATO SHEPHERD'S PIE

**Preparation Time :** 35 minutes
**Cooking Time :** 30 minutes
**Serving :** 8
**Ingredients :**
•5 potatoes, peeled and cut into chunks
•1 lb ground beef
•½ lb bulk pork sausage
•½ lb fresh mushrooms, quartered
•2 chopped carrots
•2 chopped celery ribs
•1 chopped onion
•2 garlic cloves
•½ cup of orange juice
•2 tbsp grated orange zest
•1 tbsp ground nutmeg
•¼ tbsp Worcestershire sauce
•½ tbsp salt
•½ tbsp pepper
•¼ cup Dijon mustard
•2 tbsp brown sugar

•1 tbsp rice vinegar

**Preparation :**

1.Put the potatoes in a saucepan and cover them with water.

2.Bring the potatoes to a boil then cook for 15 minutes at a reduced heat.

3.Meanwhile in a skillet, cook the beef, sausage, mushrooms, carrots, celery, onion, and garlic over medium heat for 3 minutes.

4.Drain the beef mixture.

5.Stir in the orange juice, orange zest, nutmeg, Worcestershire sauce, ¼ tablespoon salt, and ¼ tablespoon pepper into the skillet.

6.Cook the mixture until all the liquid has evaporated.

7.Set the temperature knob of the Hamilton Beach' toaster oven to bake setting.

8.Rotate the timer knob to med and allow the toaster oven to preheat to 350° F.

9.Transfer the beef mixture to 2 baking dishes.

10. Drain the potatoes and place them in a bowl.

11. Add the mustard, sugar, vinegar, and remaining salt and pepper to the bowl. Mash the potatoes until the mixture is smooth.

12. Spread the mashed potatoes over the meat mixture.

13. Set the timer to bake the potatoes pie for 30 minutes.

14. Transfer the potato pie to a serving platter. Serve and enjoy.

Serving suggestions : serve this potato pie with sauce.

Variation tip : potatoes can be replaced with sweet potatoes.

**Nutritional value per Serving :** Calories: 410 kcal, Protein: 19g, Fat: 13g, Carbs: 54g

# SPAGHETTI PIE

**Preparation Time :** 30 minutes
**Cooking Time :** 30 minutes
**Serving :** 6
**Ingredients :**
- 6 oz uncooked spaghetti
- 1 lb 90% lean ground beef
- ½ cup onion, finely chopped
- ¼ cup green pepper, chopped
- 1 cup canned diced tomatoes
- 6 oz tomato paste
- 1 tbsp dried oregano
- ¾ tbsp salt
- ½ tbsp garlic powder
- ¼ tbsp pepper
- ¼ tbsp sugar
- 2 egg white, lightly beaten
- 1 tbsp melted butter
- ¼ cup parmesan cheese, grated
- 1 cup 2% cottage cheese
- ½ cup part-skim mozzarella cheese, shredded

### Preparation :

1.Set the temperature knob of the Hamilton Beach' toaster oven to bake setting.

2.Rotate the timer knob to light and allow the toaster oven to preheat to 350° F.

3.Cook the spaghetti according to the package directions.

4.In a skillet brown the beef together with onion and green pepper over medium heat for 5 minutes.

5.Stir in the tomatoes, tomato paste, oregano, salt, garlic powder, pepper, and sugar to the skillet and remove from heat.

6.In a bowl whisk the eggs, butter, and parmesan cheese until well mixed.

7.Drain the spaghetti then add into the egg mixture and toss to coat.

8.Spread the spaghetti mixture on the bottom and upside of a pie plate.

9.Layer the cottage cheese on the spaghetti and top with the beef mixture.

10. Set the timer to bake the pie for 20 minutes.

11. When the timer has gone off, sprinkle the pie with mozzarella cheese and bake for additional 10 minutes.

12. Transfer the spaghetti pie to a serving platter.

13. Serve and enjoy.

Serving suggestions : serve this spaghetti pie with baked zucchini chips.

Variation tip : cottage cheese can be replaced with ricotta cheese.

**Nutritional value per Serving :** Calories: 348 kcal, Protein: 29g, Fat: 10g, Carbs: 33g

## 19

# BUTTERNUT SQUASH MAC AND CHEESE

**Preparation Time :** 35 minutes
**Cooking Time :** 15 minutes
**Serving :** 4
**Ingredients :**
•8 oz uncooked whole-wheat elbow macaroni
•1 butternut squash, seeded and cubed
•¼ cup plain Greek yogurt
1 cup fat-free milk
1 tbsp salt
•¼ tbsp pepper
•Dash of ground nutmeg
•1 ½ cup sharp cheddar cheese, shredded
•½ cup parmesan cheese, shredded
•½ cup soft whole wheat bread crumbs
**Preparation :**
1.Set the temperature knob of the Hamilton Beach' toaster oven to bake setting.
2.Rotate the timer knob to light and allow the toaster oven to preheat to 400° F.
3.Cook the macaroni according to the package directions.

4.Put the squash in a saucepan and cover with water.

5.Bring the squash to a boil and allow to cook for 10 minutes.

6.Put the yogurt, milk, salt, pepper, nutmeg, and drained squash in a blender and blend until a puree is formed.

7.Place the puree in the saucepan and continue heating.

8.Stir in the cheeses into the puree until they melt.

9.Drain the pasta then add into the squash mixture and toss to coat.

10. Transfer the squash into a baking dish and sprinkle with the bread crumbs.

11. Set the timer to bake the squash for 20 minutes.

12. Transfer the squash to a serving platter.

13. Serve and enjoy.

Serving suggestions : serve this squash with toppings such as bacon-cheddar shredded cheese.

Variation tip : fresh butternut can be replaced with frozen butternut

**Nutritional value per Serving :** Calories: 422 kcal, Protein: 20g, Fat: 13g, Carbs: 60g

## 20

# ASPARAGUS AND HAM STRATA

**Preparation Time :** 5 hours 10 minutes
**Cooking Time :** 1 hour
**Serving :** 6
**Ingredients :**
•5 eggs
•2 cups whole milk
•½ cup half-and-half cream
•½ tbsp salt
•¼ tbsp pepper
•⅛ tbsp ground nutmeg
•4 cups Italian bread
•1 ¼ cups Monterey jack cheese, shredded
•1 cup deli ham, cubed
•1 cup cut fresh asparagus
**Preparation :**
1.In a bowl whisk the egg, milk, cream, salt, pepper, and nutmeg until well combined.
2.Stir in 1 cup of cheese, ham, and asparagus into the egg mixture.

3.Transfer the asparagus mixture into a baking dish and refrigerate it for 5 hours.

4.Remove the strata from the refrigerator and allow to thaw for 30 minutes before cooking.

5.Set the temperature knob of the Hamilton Beach' toaster oven to bake setting.

6.Rotate the timer knob to light and allow the toaster oven to preheat to 325° F.

7.Bake the strata uncovered for 20 minutes.

8.When the timer has gone off sprinkle the remaining cheese and bake for an additional 40 minutes.

9.Transfer the strata to a serving platter.

10. Serve and enjoy.

Serving suggestions : serve this asparagus and ham with a batch of mimosa.

Variation tip : Italian bread can be replaced with French bread.

**Nutritional value per Serving :** Calories: 320 kcal, Protein: 22g, Fat: 18g, Carbs: 18g

# BEEF RECIPES

## 21

# HAMILTON BEACH" TOASTER OVEN MEATLOAF

**Preparation Time :** 10 minutes
**Cooking Time :** 1 hour
**Serving :** 4
**Ingredients :**
• 1 lb beef, ground
• ½ lb Italian sausage
• 1 egg
• 1 onion, chopped
• 1 cup milk
• 1 cup bread crumbs, dried
• Salt and pepper
• 2 tbsp brown sugar
• 2 tbsp mustard
• ⅓ cup ketchup
**Preparation :**
1.Set the temperature knob of the Hamilton Beach" toaster oven to bake setting F.
2.Rotate the timer knob (Dark) and let the toaster oven preheat to 350°F.

3.In a mixing bowl, mix ground beef, sausage, egg, onion, milk, and breadcrumbs until well combined.

4.Season with salt and pepper then pour on a foil-lined baking pan. Flatten the meatloaf.

5.In a separate mixing bowl, mix sugar, mustard, and ketchup. Pour the mixture over the meatloaf. Shape into a flat loaf of about 3 inches thick.

6.Rotate the timer knob to Stay-on setting and bake for 45 minutes or until cooked through. Serve and enjoy.

Serving suggestions : serve with your favourite side dish and veggies

Variation tip : you can use bread and crackers in place of the breadcrumbs

**Nutritional value per Serving :** Calories: 212 kcal, Protein: 19g, Fat: 12g, Carbs: 9g

# 22

# HAMILTON BEACH' TOASTER OVEN BROILED FLANK STEAK WITH HERB OIL

**Preparation Time :** 10 minutes
**Cooking Time :** 20 minutes
**Serving :** 4
**Ingredients :**
•¼ cup +2 tbsp extra virgin olive oil
•¼ cup fresh parsley, chopped
•2 tbsp red wine vinegar
•1 garlic clove
•Red pepper flakes, crushed
•Salt and pepper
•1 ½ lb flank steak
**Preparation :**
1.Potion the rack in the upper position.
2.Line the pan with a baking sheet and place the pan on the rack.
3.Set the temperature knob of the Hamilton Beach' toaster oven to broiler setting.
4.Rotate the timer knob (Dark) and let the toaster oven preheat until hot.

5.Meanwhile, mix ¼ cup oil, parsley, wine vinegar, garlic, pepper flakes, salt, and pepper in a mixing bowl. Set aside.

6.In a separate mixing bowl, mix the remaining oil, 2 tbsp salt, and 1 tbsp pepper. Rub the mixture on all sides of the steak

7.Carefully remove the hot pan from the toaster oven and place the steak at the centre.

8.Broil for 10 minutes or until well cooked.

9.Slice the steak and serve with the herb oil mixture.

Serving suggestions : Serve with sautéed veggies such as asparagus or broccoli

Variation tip : use dry herbs in place of the fresh herbs

**Nutritional value per Serving :** Calories: 169kcal, Protein: 24g, Fat: 7g, Carbs: 1g

# 23

# HAMILTON BEACH' TOASTER OVEN ITALIAN HOT DISH

**Preparation Time :** 30 minutes
**Cooking Time :** 40 minutes
**Serving :** 4
**Ingredients :**
- 1 ½ cooked multigrain bow tie pasta
- 1 lb ground beef
- 1 cup fresh mushrooms, divided
- ½ cup onion, chopped
- ½ cup green pepper
- 1 tbsp oregano
- ½ tbsp garlic powder
- ¼ tbsp onion powder
- ⅛ tbsp pepper
- 15 oz tomato sauce
- ½ cup mozzarella cheese, shredded
- 2 tbsp parmesan cheese, grated

**Preparation :**

1.Set the temperature knob of the Hamilton Beach' toaster oven to bake setting.

2.Rotate the timer knob (Med) and let the toaster oven preheat to 350°F.

3.Spray a skillet with cooking spray and cook the ground beef with ½ the mushrooms, onions, and pepper until no longer pink.

4.Stir in seasonings and tomato sauce then bring the mixture to boil. Reduce heat and let simmer while covered for 15 minutes.

5.Place the pasta in a baking dish coated with cooking spray. Top pasta with the sauce mixture, remaining mushrooms, ¼ cup mozzarella cheese, and 1 tbsp parmesan cheese.

6.Place the pan on the rack in the bottom position. Rotate the timer knob to the Stay-on setting and bake for 35 minutes.

7.Remove the pan from the toaster oven and sprinkle with the remaining cheeses.

8.Bake for additional 10 minutes or until the cheese has melted.

9.Serve and enjoy.

Serving suggestions : sprinkle with green onions and serve

Variation tip : you can omit mushrooms and add pepperoni slices

**Nutritional value per Serving :** Calories: 394 kcal, Protein: 34g, Fat: 15g, Carbs: 32g

## 24

# MOZZARELLA BAKED SPAGHETTI

**Preparation Time :** 20 minutes
**Cooking Time :** 30 minutes
**Serving :** 8
**Ingredients :**
• 8 oz spaghetti, cooked and drained
• 1 egg
• ½ cup whole milk
• ½ tbsp salt
• ½ lb ground beef
• ½ lb Italian sausage
• 1 onion, chopped
• ¼ cup green pepper
• 14 oz spaghetti sauce, meatless
• 8oz tomato sauce
• 2 cups mozzarella cheese, shredded
**Preparation :**
1.Set the temperature knob of the Hamilton Beach' toaster oven to bake setting.

2.Rotate the timer knob (light) and let the toaster oven preheat to 350°F.

3.Meanwhile, mix egg, milk, and salt in a mixing bowl. Add the drained spaghetti to the egg mixture and toss until well coated.

4.Cook beef, sausage, onion, and peppers in a skillet over medium heat until no longer pink.

5.Stir in spaghetti sauce and tomato sauce. Spoon the mixture over the spaghetti.

6.Bake for 20 minutes. Sprinkle with cheese and bake for an additional 10 minutes or until the cheese has melted.

7.Let it stand for 10 minutes before serving.

Serving suggestions : serve with your favourite salad

Variation tip : use the ground beef and omit the sausage

**Nutritional value per Serving :** Calories: 286 kcal, Protein: 17g, Fat: 11g, Carbs: 29g

# 25

# BAKE ONCE, EAT TWICE LASANGA

**Preparation Time :** 35 minutes
    **Cooking Time :** 35 minutes
    **Serving :** 12
    **Ingredients :**
    •18 lasagna noodles, cooked
    •3 lb ground beef
    •26 spaghetti sauce
    •2 eggs, beaten
    •1 ½ lb ricotta cheese
    •6 cups mozzarella cheese, shredded
    •1 tbsp parsley flakes
    •1 tbsp salt
    •½ tbsp pepper
    •18 lasagna noodles, cooked
    •1 cup parmesan cheese
    **Preparation :**
1.Set the temperature knob of the Hamilton Beach' toaster oven to bake.

2.Rotate the timer knob (Dark) and let the toaster oven preheat to 375°F.

3.Cook beef in a skillet over medium heat while breaking into crumbles. Stir in spaghetti sauce and set aside.

4.In a mixing bowl, mix eggs, ricotta cheese, 4 ½ cups mozzarella cheese, parsley flakes, salt, and pepper.

5.Drain the noodles and spread some meat sauce on a baking dish. Layer some noodles on top of the sauce.

6.layer some ricotta mixture and the meat sauce on top. Repeat the process twice and until all the ingredients are used. Top everything with parmesan cheese.

7.Rotate the timer knob to Stay-on setting and bake for 45 minutes or until cooked through.

8.Let sit for 10 minutes before serving.

Serving suggestions : serve with Caesar salad with garlic butter breadcrumbs

Variation tip : use fresh parsley instead of dried parsley and Italian seasoning

**Nutritional value per Serving :** Calories: 365 kcal, Protein: 27g, Fat: 17g, Carbs: 25g

# 26

# SPAGHETTI CASSEROLE BAKE

**Preparation Time :** 15 minutes
   **Cooking Time :** 25 minutes
   **Serving :** 2
   **Ingredients :**
- 1 ½ lb ground beef
- 1 cup green pepper, chopped
- ½ cup onion, chopped
- 1 tbsp salt
- ½ tbsp pepper
- 1 tbsp garlic
- 14 ¾ oz spaghetti in tomato sauce with cheese
- 6 oz mushrooms, sliced and drained
- 2 ¼ oz ripe olives, sliced and drained
- 2 cups cheddar cheese, shredded
- 1 cup parmesan cheese, grated

**Preparation :**

1.Set the temperature knob of the Hamilton Beach' toaster oven to bake setting.

2.Rotate the timer knob (Med) and let the toaster oven preheat to 375°F.

ALICIA MILLNER

3.Meanwhile, cook beef, green pepper, onion, salt, and pepper in a skillet over medium heat until the meat is no longer pink.

4.Add garlic and cook for 1 more minute then stir in the spaghetti, mushrooms, and olives.

5.Transfer the mixture into two greased baking dishes. Sprinkle with cheese.

6.Place the baking dish on the rack in the bottom position and bake for 1 hour while covered.

7.Uncover and bake for an additional 20 minutes.

8.Serve and enjoy.

Serving suggestions : serve the casserole with salad

Variation tip : you can replace spaghetti with pasta then omit mushrooms and olives

**Nutritional value per Serving :** Calories: 342 kcal, Protein: 27g, Fat: 20g, Carbs: 13g

27
___

# LASAGNA ROLLS

**Preparation Time :** 25 minutes
**Cooking Time :** 10 minutes
**Serving :** 6
**Ingredients :**
•6 lasagna noodles
•1 lb ground beef
•14 oz spaghetti sauce
•2 cups part-skim mozzarella cheese, shredded
**Preparation :**
1.Set the temperature knob of the Hamilton Beach' toaster oven to bake setting.

2.Rotate the timer knob to light and preheat the toaster oven to 350° F.

3.Cook the noodles according to the package directions.

4.Meanwhile, brown the beef in a skillet over medium heat.

5.Drain the beef and stir in the spaghetti sauce.

6.Drain the lasagna noodles.

7.On each noodle spread ¼ cup of the beef sauce and sprinkle the noodles with 2 tablespoons of mozzarella cheese.

8.Roll up the noodles and place them in a baking dish with the seam side down.

9.Top the lasagna rolls with the remaining beef sauce and cheese.

10. Bake the lasagna rolls for 10 minutes.

11. Transfer the lasagna rolls to a serving platter.

12. Serve and enjoy.

Serving suggestions : serve these lasagna rolls with chilli flakes and basil.

Variation tip : mozzarella cheese can be replaced with other cheese.

**Nutritional value per Serving :** Calories: 377 kcal, Protein: 28g, Fat: 18g, Carbs: 26g

# CHIPOTLE MAC AND CHEESE

**Preparation Time :** 35 minutes
**Cooking Time :** 30 minutes
**Serving :** 8
**Ingredients :**
- 16 oz spiral pasta
- 2 lb beef, ground
- 2 chopped onions
- 2 chopped green peppers
- 3 minced garlic cloves
- 28 oz crushed tomatoes
- 11 oz condensed cheddar cheese soup
- ½ cup 2% milk
- 1 chopped chipotle pepper in adobo sauce
- 2 tbsp chilli powder
- 1 tbsp ground cumin
- 1 tbsp cayenne pepper
- 1 tbsp dried oregano
- ½ tbsp salt
- ¼ tbsp black pepper
- 2 cups Monterey jack cheese, shredded

**Preparation :**

1.Set the temperature knob of the Hamilton Beach' toaster oven to bake setting.

2.Rotate the timer knob to light and preheat the toaster oven to 350° F.

3.Cook the spiral pasta according to the package directions.

4.Meanwhile, cook the beef, onions, green pepper, and garlic over medium heat in a skillet until the beef is browned.

5.Add the tomatoes, soup, milk, chipotle pepper, chilli powder, cumin, cayenne pepper, oregano, salt, and black pepper to the skillet and stir to mix them.

6.Allow the beef mixture to boil for about 15 minutes until the sauce is thickened.

7.Drain the pasta and stir into the beef mixture.

8.Pour the pasta mixture into 2 casserole dishes and cover them.

9.Place the casserole dishes in the toaster oven and bake them for 20 minutes.

10. When the timer has gone off, uncover the casserole dishes and bake them for an additional 10 minutes.

11. Transfer the chipotle Mac and cheese to a serving platter.

12. Serve and enjoy

Serving suggestions : serve this chipotle Mac and cheese with salad.

Variation tip : Monterey jack cheese can be replaced with your favourite cheese.

**Nutritional value per Serving :** Calories: 461 kcal, Protein: 26g, Fat: 35g, Carbs: 8g

# 29

# VEGETABLE AND BEEF STUFFED RED PEPPERS

**Preparation Time :** 35 minutes
**Cooking Time :** 40 minutes
**Serving :** 6
**Ingredients :**
•6 sweet red peppers
•1 lb 90% lean ground beef
•1 tbsp olive oil
•1 chopped zucchini
•1 chopped yellow summer squash
•1 finely chopped onion
•⅓ cup green pepper, finely chopped
•2 cups fresh spinach, coarsely chopped
•4 minced garlic cloves
•1 cup ready to serve wild rice
•8 oz tomato sauce
•½ cup part-skim mozzarella cheese, shredded
•¼ tbsp salt
•3 slices reduced-fat provolone cheese
**Preparation :**

1.Set the temperature knob of the Hamilton Beach' toaster oven to bake setting.

2.Rotate the timer knob to light and preheat the toaster oven to 350° F.

3.Cut the red pepper tops and discard. Remove the seeds.

4.In a stockpot, cook the peppers in boiling water for 3 minutes.

5.Drain the peppers and rinse with cold water then set aside.

6.In a skillet brown the beef for 6 minutes over medium heat.

7.Transfer the beef to a dish and pour off the drippings.

8.In the same skillet, heat oil then sauté zucchini, yellow squash, onion, and green pepper for 5 minutes.

9.Stir in spinach and garlic and cook for 5 minutes.

10. Stir in the beef, rice, tomato sauce, mozzarella cheese, and salt to the skillet. Stuff the beef mixture into the red peppers and place them in a baking dish. Cover the dish. Bake the stuffed peppers for 35 minutes.

11. When the timer has gone off, uncover the baking dish and top the peppers with provolone cheese.

12. Place the stuffed peppers back in the toaster oven and allow the cheese to melt for about 5 minutes.

13. Transfer the stuffed peppers to a serving platter. Serve and enjoy.

Serving suggestions : serve these stuffed peppers with greens beans.

Variation tip : spinach can be replaced with fresh mushrooms.

**Nutritional value per Serving :** Calories: 287kcal, Protein: 23g, Fat: 13g, Carbs: 21g

# 30

# SALT AND PEPPER BEEF ROAST

**Preparation Time :** 25 minutes

**Cooking Time :** 2 hours

**Serving :** 15

**Ingredients :**

•6 lb tied beef cross rib roast, boned

•¼ cup of salt

•¼ cup of sugar

•1 ½ tbsp salt

•2 tbsp coarse ground pepper

•½ cup horseradish

**Preparation :**

1.Rinse the beef and dry it with a paper towel.

2.Mix ¼ cup salt and sugar in a bowl.

3.Rub the salt and sugar mixture over the beef and allow to chill for 4 hours covered.

4.Rinse the beef and dry it with a paper towel.

5.In a shallow dish mix 1 ½ tablespoon salt, pepper, and horseradish.

6.Place the beef on a rack and rub the horseradish mixture.

7.Transfer the beef to a baking pan.

8.Set the temperature knob of the Hamilton Beach' toaster oven to bake setting.

9.Rotate the timer knob to dark and preheat the toaster oven to 400° F.

10. Place the beef roast in the toaster oven and allow it to bake for 2 hours.

11. Transfer the beef roast to a serving cutting board.

12. Cut the beef roast into thin slices.

13. Serve and enjoy.

Serving suggestions : serve this beef roast with savory green beans.

Variation tip : pepper can be replaced with desired herbs.

**Nutritional value per Serving :** Calories: 267 kcal, Protein: 20g, Fat: 19g, Carbs: 1g

# PORK RECIPES

# 31

# HAMILTON BEACH' TOASTER OVEN BROILED PORK CHOPS

**Preparation Time :** 14 minutes
**Cooking Time :** 12 minutes
**Serving :** 8
**Ingredients :**
•32 oz Boneless pork Chops
•2 tbsp olive oil
•1 tbsp garlic powder
•1 tbsp onion powder
•Salt and pepper to taste
**Preparation :**
1.Pat the pork chops dry with a paper towel then toss them with oil, garlic powder, onion, salt, and pepper.

2.Arrange the pork chops on a rimmed baking sheet. Place the baking sheet on the rack in the higher position.

3.Set the temperature knob of the Hamilton Beach' toaster oven to broiler setting at 450°F.

4.Broil for 12 minutes or until the internal temperature reaches 145°F.

Serving suggestions : scrve with fried apples and glazed carrots

Variation tip : You can substitute garlic powder with fresh garlic, onion powder with fresh onions.

**Nutritional value per Serving :** Calories: 168 kcal, Protein: 21g, Fat: 9g, Carbs: 1g

# 32

# HAMILTON BEACH' TOASTER OVEN PORK LOIN

**Preparation Time :** 20 minutes
    **Cooking Time :** 1 hour 20 minutes
    **Serving :** 8
    **Ingredients :**
• 3 garlic cloves, minced
• 1 tbsp rosemary, dried
• Salt and pepper
• 2 lb pork loin
• ¼ cup olive oil
• ½ cup white wine
    **Preparation :**
1.Set the temperature knob of the Hamilton Beach' toaster oven to bake setting.

2.Rotate the timer knob (Med) and let the toaster oven preheat to 350°F.

3.Mix garlic cloves, rosemary, salt, and pepper to make a paste. Pierce the meat with a knife then press the garlic paste into the cuts.

4.Rub the meat with the remaining paste and more oil. Place the pork on a baking pan and place it on the rack.

5.Rotate the timer knob to the Stay-on setting and bake for 1 hour or until the internal temperature reaches 145°F.

6.Transfer the pork from the pan to a platter.

7.Het wine in the pan while stirring to loosen any food bites at the bottom. Serve the pork with the pan juices.

Serving suggestions : Serve with buttered herb rice and gravy

Variation tip : Use white wine vinegar and chicken stock instead of white wine.

**Nutritional value per Serving :** Calories: 238 kcal, Protein: 18g, Fat: 16g, Carbs: 1g

## 33

# CAJUN PORK CHOPS

**Preparation Time :** 10 minutes
**Cooking Time :** 40 minutes
**Serving :** 4
**Ingredients :**
•Vegetable oil cooking spray
•1 ½ tbsp garlic powder
•1 ½ tbsp paprika
•1 tbsp cayenne pepper
•1 tbsp salt
•1 tbsp dried thyme
•½ tbsp white pepper
•¼ tbsp black pepper
•⅓ cup white germ
•¼ cup bread crumbs
•½ cup milk, reduced fat
•1 egg
•4 center-cut loin chops (6 oz each)
•⅔ cup all-purpose flour
**Preparation :**
1.Place the Hamilton Beach' toaster broiler pan in the upper

position and Set the temperature knob of the Hamilton Beach' toaster oven to broil setting at 375°F.

2.Coat the broiler pan with cooking spray and add a ¼ cup of water to the drip tray.

3.I a mixing bowl, combine garlic powder and the next 6 ingredients. Divide the mixture into halves and reserve each in a pan.

4.Add white germ and bread crumbs to one of the pans. Mix well to combine.

5.Combine milk and egg in a separate mixing bowl until well mixed.

6.Place flour in another mixing bowl. Dredge each pork chop in spice, then in flour, in milk mixture, and finally in white germ mixture.

7.Arrange the chops in a single layer on the pan. Broil for 20 minutes.

8.Turn the chops and broil for an additional 20 minutes or until the internal temperature reaches 165°F.

Serving suggestions : serve with lemon wedges, a sprinkle of rosemary and lettuce leaves

Variation tip : use regular cooking oil in place of vegetable oil cooking spray

**Nutritional value per Serving** : Calories: 681 kcal, Protein: 63g, Fat: 14g, Carbs: 24g

# 34

# PORK TENDERLOIN WITH CARROTS

**Preparation Time :** 10 minutes
**Cooking Time :** 25 minutes
**Serving :** 5
**Ingredients :**
•1 lb pork tenderloin
•1 tbsp steak seasoning blend
•2 carrots, sliced
•2 parsnips, sliced
•½ sweet onion, cut into thin wedges
•1 tbsp olive oil
•Salt and pepper to taste
•½ cup apricot jam
•1 tbsp balsamic vinegar
**Preparation :**
1.Place the rack at the bottom position of the Hamilton Beach' toaster oven.

2.Rotate the timer knob (Med) and let the toaster oven preheat to 425°F.

3.Spray a baking pan with cooking spray then place the pork at the centre of the pan. Sprinkle the meat with seasoning blend.

4.In a mixing bowl, mix carrots, parsnips, and sweet onion. Add oil, salt, and pepper. Stir until the veggies are well coated.

5.Arrange the vegetables around the pork and place the baking pan in the toaster oven. Bake for 20 minutes.

6.Meanwhile, mix apricot jam and vinegar in a mixing bowl. Spoon half of the mixture over the pork.

7.Bake for an additional 10 minutes or until the internal temperature reaches 160°F.

Serving suggestions : serve with more apricot jam and vinegar sauce and some sautéed broccoli.

Variation tip : use potatoes in place of parsnips

**Nutritional value per Serving :** Calories: 366 kcal, Protein: 29g, Fat: 18g, Carbs: 21g

# 35

# PORK BELLY AND RED CABBAGE

**Preparation Time :** 15 minutes
**Cooking Time :** 1 hour
**Serving :** 1
**Ingredients :**
•Pork belly
•Salt to taste
•Black peppercorns
•½ red cabbage, shredded
•2 tbsp Queensland nut oil
•1 stick butter
**Preparation :**
1.Rub salt on the pork belly then until well seasoned.
2.Layout the shredded cabbage on the baking sheet lined with foil.
3.Place the baking sheet with cabbage in the Hamilton Beach' toaster oven and place the rack in a higher position.
4.Set the temperature knob of the Hamilton Beach' toaster oven to the baking setting at 450°F.
5.Place butter on the cabbage and the pork belly on the rack.

6.Cook for 20 minutes. Reduce heat to 400°F and cook for an additional 25 minutes.

7.Let rest for 5 minutes before serving the pork belly on top of the cabbage.

Serving suggestions : Serve with pasta and tomato sauce.

Variation tip : Use Chinese cabbage in place of the red cabbage

**Nutritional value per Serving :** Calories: 232 kcal, Protein: 26g, Fat: 19g, Carbs: 3g

# 36

# BROILED PORK CHOPS WITH HOT CHERRY PEPPER

**Preparation Time :** 10 minutes
**Cooking Time :** 25 minutes
**Serving :** 4
**Ingredients :**
- 4 pork chops
- 1 tbsp seas salt
- 1 tbsp black pepper
- 6 oz hot cherry peppers
- 3 garlic cloves, smashed
- ½ onion

**Preparation :**

1.Pat dry the pork chops with a paper towel then rub them with salt and pepper.

2.Layer the chops on a lined baking tray. Sound the chops with cherry peppers, garlic, and onions.

3.Set the tray in the higher position and Set the temperature knob of the Hamilton Beach' toaster oven to the broiling setting at 450°F.

4.Broil for 12 minutes on each side or until the internal temperature reaches 150°F.

5.Serve and enjoy.

Serving suggestions :

Variation tip :

**Nutritional value per Serving :** Calories: 40 kcal, Protein: 2g, Fat: 1g, Carbs: 6g

# 37

# BAKED PORK CHOPS

**Preparation Time :** 20 minutes
**Cooking Time :** 20 minutes
**Serving :** 4
**Ingredients :**
•1 ½ cups panko
•5 tbsp vegetable oil
•3 tbsp parmesan, grated
•2 tbsp dried Italian seasoning
•Kosher salt to taste
•Ground black pepper to taste
•4 bone-in pork chops, ¾ inch
•1 tbsp water
**Preparation :**
1.Set the temperature knob of the Hamilton Beach' toaster oven to bake setting.
2.Rotate the timer knob to dark and allow the toaster oven to preheat to 450° F.
3.In a bowl mix the panko, oil, parmesan, Italian seasoning, salt, and pepper until well combined.
4.Mix the pork with water in a bowl.

5.Add the pork chops to the seasoning mixture and toss to coat.

6.Place the pork on the baking sheet and put it in the toaster oven.

7.Set the timer to bake the pork for 20minutes.

8.Transfer the pork chops to a serving platter.

9.Serve and enjoy.

Serving suggestions : serve these pork chops with lemon wedges.

Variation tip : vegetable oil can be replaced with olive oil.

**Nutritional value per Serving :** Calories: 545 kcal, Protein: 43g, Fat: 35g, Carbs: 12g

# 38

# BROILED BONELESS PORK CHOPS

**Preparation Time :** 10 minutes
  **Cooking Time :** 10 minutes
  **Serving :** 4
  **Ingredients :**
  •4 pork chops, boneless ¾ inch thick
  •1 tbsp olive oil
  •1 tbsp salt
  •½ tbsp paprika
  •Black pepper to taste
  •4 tbsp pesto
  •4 slices mozzarella cheese
  •1 thinly sliced tomato
  **Preparation :**
  1.Cut the pork chops down in the middle to form a flap.
  2.Rub the pork with olive oil, salt, paprika, and black pepper.
  3.Fill each of the pork chops with 1 tablespoon of pesto, a slice of mozzarella cheese, and 3 slices of tomatoes.
  4.Place the pork chops on a baking tray.
  5.Set the temperature knob of the Hamilton Beach' toaster oven to broil setting.

6.Rotate the timer knob to dark and broil the pork chops for 20 minutes at 450° F.

7.Transfer the pork chops to a serving platter.

8.Serve and enjoy.

Serving suggestions : serve these pork chops with lemon wedges.

Variation tip : mozzarella cheese can be replaced with favourite cheese.

**Nutritional value per Serving :** Calories: 387 kcal, Protein: 36g, Fat: 24g, Carbs: 3g

# 39

# BAKED BONELESS PORK CHOPS

**Preparation Time :** 15 minutes
**Cooking Time :** 20 minutes
**Serving :** 6
**Ingredients :**
• $\frac{3}{4}$ cup ketchup
• $\frac{3}{4}$ cup of water
• 2 tbsp white vinegar
• 1 tbsp Worcestershire sauce
• 2 tbsp brown sugar
• 1 tbsp salt
• $\frac{1}{2}$ tbsp paprika
• $\frac{1}{2}$ tbsp chilli powder
• $\frac{1}{8}$ tbsp pepper
• 6 boneless pork loin chops, $\frac{3}{4}$ inch thick
**Preparation :**
1.Set the temperature knob of the Hamilton Beach' toaster oven to bake setting.

2.Rotate the timer knob to dark and allow the toaster oven to preheat to 450° F.

3.Mix the ketchup, water, vinegar, Worcestershire sauce, sugar, salt, paprika, chilli powder, and pepper in a saucepan.

4.Bring the seasoning mixture to a boil and allow simmering for 5 minutes ensuring that you stir occasionally.

5.Reserve half the sauce to serve with the pork chops.

6.Add the pork chops to the remaining sauce and toss to coat.

7.Place the coated chops in the baking tray and bake them for 20 minutes.

8.Transfer the pork chops to a serving platter and drizzle them with the remaining sauce.

9.Serve and enjoy.

Serving suggestions : Serve the pork chops with rice.

Variation tip : the sauce can be replaced with your favourite sauce.

**Nutritional value per Serving :** Calories: 190 kcal, Protein: 22g, Fat: 7g, Carbs: 10g

# 40

# GOLDEN BAKED PORK CUTLETS

**Preparation Time :** 15 minutes
    **Cooking Time :** 20 minutes
    **Serving :** 4
    **Ingredients :**
    •1 lb trimmed pork tenderloin,
    •½ cup dry breadcrumbs
    •1 tbsp sugar
    •½ tbsp paprika
    •½ tbsp onion powder
    •½ tbsp salt
    •4 tbsp canola oil
    •4 tbsp cornstarch
    •1 egg white, lightly beaten
    **Preparation :**
    1.Set the temperature knob of the Hamilton Beach' toaster oven to bake setting.
    2.Rotate the timer knob to med and allow the toaster oven to preheat to 400° F.
    3.Slice the pork into 4 long fillets.

4.In a bowl mix the breadcrumbs, sugar, paprika, onion powder, and salt until well combined.

5.Drizzle oil in the breadcrumb mixture and mix well using a fork.

6.Sprinkle the pork with cornstarch, then dip in the egg and coat with bread crumb mixture.

7.Place the pork on a baking sheet then put it in the toaster oven.

8.Set the timer to bake the pork for 20 minutes.

9.Transfer the pork to a serving platter.

10. Serve and enjoy.

Serving suggestions : serve these pork cutlets with greens beans.

Variation tip : bread crumbs can be replaced with whole wheat flour.

**Nutritional value per Serving :** Calories: 220 kcal, Protein: 26g, Fat: 7g, Carbs: 11g

# LAMB RECIPES

# 41

# HERB TOASTED LAMB CHOPS

**Preparation Time :** 10 minutes
**Cooking Time :** 25 minutes
**Serving :** 4
**Ingredients :**
•4 garlic cloves, pressed
•1 tbsp thyme leaves, crushed
•1 tbsp rosemary leaves
•2 tbsp kosher salt
•2 tbsp extra virgin olive oil
•6 1 ¼ inch thick lamb chops

**Preparation :**

1.In a mixing bowl, mix garlic cloves, thyme, rosemary, salt, and 1 tbsp oil. Add the lamb chops and mix until well coated.

2.Let sit to marinate for at least 30 minutes.

3.Heat the remaining 1 tbsp of oil in a skillet and cook until browned.

4.Transfer the lamb to the Toaster oven tray.

5.Set the temperature knob of the Hamilton Beach' toaster oven to Toast setting at 400°F.

6.Toast the lamb for 10 minutes or until the desired doneness is achieved.

7.Let the lamb rest before serving.

Serving suggestions : serve with buttered egg noodles and sautéed kale

Variation tip : you can use regular oil in place of extra virgin olive oil

**Nutritional value per Serving :** Calories: 258 kcal, Protein: 26g, Fat: 17g, Carbs: 0g

# 42

## CLASSIC RACK OF LAMB IN THE HAMILTON BEACH' TOASTER OVEN

**Preparation Time :** 10 minutes
**Cooking Time :** 25 minutes
**Serving :** 3
**Ingredients :**
- 2 lb rack of lamb
- 2 tbsp fresh rosemary, chopped
- 2 garlic cloves
- 1 tbsp fresh thyme, chopped
- Salt and pepper
- 2 tbsp extra virgin olive oil

**Preparation :**

1.In a mixing bowl, mix rosemary, garlic, and thyme. Sprinkle salt and pepper. Rub the mixture on the lamb until well coated.

2.Place the lamb in a resealable bag with oil. Massage it until it's well coated with oil.

3.Place the bag in a container to catch any leaks. Let marinate overnight for at least 2 hours.

4.Arrange the rack of lamb in the middle of the toaster oven tray. Score the fat and sprinkle with more salt and pepper.

5.Wrap the bones with foil and ensure the lamb has been placed on the bone side down.

6.Set the temperature knob of the Hamilton Beach' toaster oven to Toast setting at 450°F.

7.Cook for 10 minutes or until the surface is nicely browned.

8.Reduce the temperature to 300°F and cook for an additional 20 minutes.

9.Remove the lamb from the toaster oven and let rest before serving.

Serving suggestions : serve with roasted or sautéed veggies

Variation tip : you can replace the fresh herbs with dry herbs

**Nutritional value per Serving :** Calories: 335 kcal, Protein: 21g, Fat: 26g, Carbs: 2g

## 43

# TOASTED RACK OF LAMB

**Preparation Time :** 20 minutes
**Cooking Time :** 20 minutes
**Serving :** 4
**Ingredients :**
•½ cup bread crumbs, fresh
•2 tbsp garlic, minced
•2 tbsp fresh rosemary, chopped
•1 tbsp salt
•¼ black pepper
•2 tbsp olive oil
•1 rack of lamb, trimmed and frenched
•1 tbsp salt
•1 tbsp black pepper
•2 tbsp olive oil
•1 tbsp Dijon mustard
**Preparation :**
1.In a mixing bowl, mix bread crumbs, garlic, rosemary, salt, and ¼ tbsp pepper. Add oil and toss until the mixture is moistened. Set aside.

2.Season the lamb with salt and pepper. Heat 2 tbsp olive oil in a skillet and sear lamb for 2 minutes.

3.Brush the lamb with Dijon mustard then roll it in the bread crumbs mixture and cover the bones with foil.

4.Arrange them on a tray with bone side down.

5.Set the temperature knob of the Hamilton Beach' toaster oven to Toast setting at 450°F.

6.Toast the rack of lamb for 18 minutes. Let it rest for 5 minutes while loosely covered before serving. Enjoy.

Serving suggestions : serve with sautéed carrots, broccoli, and your favourite side dish.

Variation tip : you can add a splash of balsamic vinegar and Worcestershire sauce. Omit salt and use Italian seasoned breadcrumbs.

**Nutritional value per Serving :** Calories: 481 kcal, Protein: 22, Fat: 41g, Carbs: 6g

## 44

# BROILED ROSEMARY LAMB CHOPS

Preparation Time :10 minutes

**Cooking Time :** 25 minutes

**Serving :** 4

**Ingredients :**

•6 lamb chops

•3 tbsp olive oil

•2 tbsp sea salt

•½ tbsp black peppercorns

•4 garlic cloves, cut in half

•12 springs fresh rosemary

**Preparation :**

1.In a mixing bowl, add lamb chops, then massage it with oil, salt, and pepper.

2.Place the chops on a greased baking pan. Stick the garlic cloves into the chops.

3.Roll rosemary springs between tour hands to release oil then place them on both sides of the chops.

4.Place the baking pan on the rack in the upper position of the Hamilton Beach' toaster oven.

5.Set the temperature knob of the toaster oven to broil setting at 450°F.

6.Broil for 10 minutes or until the internal temperature reaches 125°F. Let the chops rest before serving.

Serving suggestions : serve with your choice of sautéed veggies

Variation tip : use avocado oil in place of olive oil

**Nutritional value per Serving :** Calories: 220 kcal, Protein: 16g, Fat: 16g, Carbs: 2g

# 45

# LEG OF LAMB

**Preparation Time :** 10 minutes

**Cooking Time :** 2 hours

**Serving :** 9

**Ingredients :**

•4 garlic cloves, sliced

•Dried oregano

•Salt and black pepper to taste

•6 ½ lb leg of lamb

•2 tbsp lemon juice

•2 tbsp olive oil

**Preparation :**

1.Set the temperature knob of the Hamilton Beach' toaster oven to bake setting.

2.Rotate the timer knob (Dark) and let the toaster oven preheat to 350°F.

3.In a mixing bowl, toss garlic, oregano, salt, and pepper.

4.Score the lamb and rub the garlic mixture on the scores.

5.Rub the lemon juice and olive oil on the lamb then wrap it with foil. Brush the foil with oil and place it on a baking pan.

6.Rotate the timer knob to the Stay-on setting and bake for 2 hours or until the internal temperature reaches 140°F.

7.Let the lamb rest for 5 minutes before serving.

Serving suggestions : Serve with the cooking juices and sautéed veggies.

Variation tip : serve with sautéed carrots, peppers, and broccoli

**Nutritional value per Serving :** Calories: 260 kcal, Protein: 20g, Fat:19, Carbs: 1g

# 46

# LAMB WITH ROSEMARY AND GARLIC

**Preparation Time :** 10 minutes
   **Cooking Time :** 25 minutes
   **Serving :** 4
   **Ingredients :**
   •3 lb lamb, trimmed
   •1 tbsp fresh rosemary
   •3 garlic cloves, minced
   •1 tbsp sea salt
   **Preparation :**
   1.Set the temperature knob of the Hamilton Beach' toaster oven to bake.

   2.Rotate the timer knob ( Dark) and let the toaster oven preheat to 450°F.

   3.Secure the lamb with a heavy string at an interval of 1 inch.

   4.Rub the meat with rosemary and garlic cloves. Place it on a broiling pan.

   5.Insert a thermometer into the thickest part of the meat and place the pan on the rack at the bottom position.

   6.Rotate the timer knob to Stay-on setting and bake for 1 hour and 15 minutes or until the internal temperature reaches 140°F.

7.Sprinkle with sea salt, cover with a foil loosely and let it rest for 10 minutes.

8.Remove the string before slicing. Enjoy.

Serving suggestions : Serve with salad, sautéed vegetables, or tzatziki sauce

Variation tip : use garlic powder in place of minced garlic

**Nutritional value per Serving :** Calories: 165 kcal, Protein: 24g, Fat: 7g, Carbs: 1g

# 47

# LAMB LOIN CHOPS

**Preparation Time :** 10 minutes
    **Cooking Time :** 20 minutes
    **Serving :** 8
    **Ingredients :**
    •8 lamb loin chops
    •¼ cup olive oil
    •1 tbsp salt
    •¼ tbsp black pepper
    •1 tbsp garlic powder
    •½ tbsp thyme
    •1 tbsp oil
    **Preparation :**
1.Set the temperature knob of the Hamilton Beach' toaster oven to bake setting.

2.Rotate the timer knob to med and allow the toaster oven to preheat to 400° F.

3.Meanwhile, put the lamb chops in a bowl and season with ¼ cup oil, salt, black pepper, garlic, and thyme.

4.Pour 1 tablespoon of oil into a skillet and heat over medium heat.

5.Brown the lamb chops for 3 minutes.

6.Place the lamb chops on the baking tray and bake for 20 minutes.

7.Transfer the lamb chops to a serving platter.

8.Serve and enjoy.

Serving suggestions : serve these lamb chops with salads and potatoes.

Variation tip : the garlic powder can be replaced with fresh minced garlic.

**Nutritional value per Serving :** Calories: 411 kcal, Protein: 18g, Fat: 36g, Carbs: 0g

# 48

# HAMILTON BEACH' TOASTER OVEN LAMB CHOPS

Preparation Time :1 hour 30 minutes

Cooking Time :30 minutes

**Serving :**4

**Ingredients :**

•Two 1 lb racks of lamb

•Kosher salt

•Cracked black pepper

•⅓ cup olive oil and more for searing

•1 tbsp fresh rosemary, chopped

•6 garlic cloves, smashed

•Juice of 1 lemon

•3 tbsp Dijon mustard

•2 tbsp honey

•⅓ cup panko breadcrumbs

•⅓ cup parmesan, grated

•2 tbsp fresh parsley, chopped

•1 tbsp fresh chives, thinly sliced

**Preparation :**

1.Put the lamb in a resealable bag and sprinkle it with salt and pepper.

2.In a bowl mix ⅓ cup oil, rosemary, garlic, lemon juice, salt, and pepper until well combined.

3.Marinate the lamb and allow it to sit for 1 hour.

4.Set the temperature knob of the Hamilton Beach' toaster oven to bake setting.

5.Rotate the timer knob to dark and allow the toaster oven to preheat to 400° F. In a bowl mix the mustard and honey.

6.In another bowl add the breadcrumbs, parmesan, parsley, and chives then toss to mix.

7.Pour oil into a skillet and heat over medium heat.

8.Sear each side of the lamb for 3 minutes and transfer to a sheet tray.

9.Brush the lamb with the honey mixture then coat with breadcrumbs mixture.

10. Put the lamb in the baking tray and bake for 30 minutes.

11. Transfer the lamb to a chopping board and allow it to cool for 15 minutes.

12. Cut the lamb into chops. Serve and enjoy

Serving suggestions : serve these lamb chops with sauteed veggies.

Variation tip : seasoning herbs can be replaced with the desired herbs.

**Nutritional value per Serving :** Calories: 388 kcal, Protein: 36g, Fat: 21g, Carbs: 16g

## 49

---

# BAKED LAMB CHOPS

**Preparation Time :** 10 minutes
**Cooking Time :** 30 minutes
**Serving :**4
**Ingredients :**
• 16 lamb chops
• ½ tbsp salt
• ½ tbsp black pepper
• 1 tbsp olive oil
**Preparation :**
1. Set the temperature knob of the Hamilton Beach' toaster oven to bake setting.
2. Rotate the timer knob to med and allow the toaster oven to preheat to 400° F.
3. Season the lamb chops with salt and pepper.
4. Pour oil into a pan and sear both sides of the lamb chops.
5. Transfer the chops to the baking tray and bake for 30 minutes.
6. Transfer the lamb chops to a serving platter.
7. Serve and enjoy.

Serving suggestions : serve these lamb chops with sautéed rice.

Variation tip : use of black pepper is optional.

**Nutritional value per Serving :** Calories: 764 kcal, Protein: 84g, Fat: 42g, Carbs: 3g

# 50

# ROAST LAMB WITH ROSEMARY AND GARLIC

Preparation Time :5 minutes

Cooking Time :1 hour 15 minutes

**Serving :**8

**Ingredients :**

•3 lb boned leg of lamb

•1 tbsp fresh rosemary, chopped

•3 minced garlic cloves

•1 tbsp sea salt

**Preparation :**

1.Set the temperature knob of the Hamilton Beach' toaster oven to broil setting.

2.Rotate the timer knob to med and allow the toaster oven to preheat for 5 minutes at 450° F.

3.Meanwhile, rub the lamb with rosemary and garlic.

4.Place the lamb on the baking pan.

5.Set the timer to broil the lamb for 1 hour 15 minutes.

6.Transfer the lamb to a chopping board and sprinkle it with salt.

7.Allow to cool for 10 minutes before slicing.

8.Serve and enjoy.

Serving suggestions : Serve the lamb with tzatziki sauce.

Variation tip : additional herbs may be used if desired.

**Nutritional value per Serving :** Calories: 165 kcal, Protein: 24g, Fat: 7g, Carbs: 1g

# CHICKEN AND TURKEY RECIPES

# 51

# BBQ AND RANCH CHICKEN PIZZA

Preparation Time :10 minutes

Cooking Time :20 minutes

**Serving :**8

**Ingredients :**

•16 oz crescent rolls, refrigerated

•$\frac{1}{2}$ cup hickory smoke-flavoured BBQ sauce

•$\frac{1}{4}$ cup ranch salad dressing

•3 cups chicken breasts, cooked

•2 cups pizza cheese blend, shredded

**Preparation :**

1.Set the temperature knob of the Hamilton Beach' toaster oven to bake.

2.Rotate the timer knob and let the toaster oven preheat to 375°F.

3.Unroll the crescent rolls and press it on the bottom and up the slides of a greased baking pan. Press the perforations to seal.

4.Place the baking pan in the toaster oven and bake for 10 minutes.

5.Meanwhile, mix $\frac{1}{4}$ cup BBQ sauce and salad dressing. Spread the mixture over the crust.

6.In another bowl toss chicken with the remaining BBQ sauce. Arrange the chicken over the top.

7.Sprinkle with cheese and bake for 20 minutes or until the crust is golden brown and the cheese has melted.

Serving suggestions : serve with a hot cup of tea

Variation tip : You can use the homemade sauce in place of BBQ sauce.

**Nutritional value per Serving** : Calories:190 kcal, Protein: 10g, Fat: 3g, Carbs: 22g

# 52

# CHICKEN TATER BAKE

**Preparation Time :** 20 minutes
**Cooking Time :** 35 minutes
**Serving :** 6
**Ingredients :**
•2 cans 10 ¾ oz each cream of chicken soup, condensed
•½ cup milk
•¼ cup butter, cubed
•3 cups cooked chicken, cubed
•16 oz peas, and carrots
•1 ½ cup cheddar cheese, shredded
•32 oz Tater Tots, frozen
**Preparation :**
1.In a saucepan over medium heat, mix soup, milk, and butter. Remove from heat and stir in chicken, peas, carrots, and 1 cup cheese.
2.Transfer the mixture to a greased baking pan and top with Tater Tots.
3.Set the temperature knob of the Hamilton Beach' toaster oven to bake at 400°F
4.Rotate the timer knob and bake for 25 minutes.

5.Sprinkle with ¼ cup cheese and bake for an additional 5 minutes.

6.Serve and enjoy.

Serving suggestions : serve topped with parsley.

Variation tip : use 1 can cream of chicken soup and 1 can cream of mushroom soup in place of 2 cans cream of chicken soup.

**Nutritional value per Serving :** Calories: 356 kcal, Protein: 18g, Fat: 21g, Carbs: 29g

# 53

# CHICKEN CLUB PIZZA

**Preparation Time :** 10 minutes
   **Cooking Time :** 20 minutes
   **Serving :** 6
   **Ingredients :**
•8 oz crescent rolls
•2 tbsp sesame seeds
•¼ cup mayonnaise
•1 tbsp dried basil
•¼ tbsp grated lemon zest
•1 cup Monterey jack cheese, shredded
•4 oz deli chicken, cut into strips
•6 bacon strips, cooked and crumbled
• 2 plum tomatoes, sliced
•½ cup Swiss cheese, shredded
**Preparation :**
1.Set the temperature knob of the Hamilton Beach' toaster oven to bake.

2.Rotate the timer knob and let the toaster oven preheat to 375°F.

3.Unroll crescent dough and separate them into 8 triangles. Arrange the pieces on a greased pizza pan.

4.Press the dough onto the pan to form the crust then seal the seams.

5.Sprinkle sesame seeds and bake for 10 minutes or until the edges are lightly browned.

6.In a mixing bowl, mix mayo, basil, and lemon zest. Spread the mixture over the crust.

7.Top with Monterey jack cheese, deli chicken, bacon, tomatoes, and swiss cheese.

8.Bake for an additional 12 minutes or until the crust is golden brown and cheese has melted.

Serving suggestions : serve with salad and sauce

Variation tip : crescent rolls can be replaced with Italian Pizza Crust

**Nutritional value per Serving :** Calories: 387 kcal, Protein: 16g, Fat: 28g, Carbs: 17g

# 54

# CHICKEN TATER TOT CASSEROLE

**Preparation Time :** 15 minutes
**Cooking Time :** 45 minutes
**Serving :** 6
**Ingredients :**
- 2 cans cream of chicken soup
- 1 cup sour cream
- ½ cup milk
- 2 tbsp Worcestershire sauce
- 1 tbsp lemon juice
- 8 slices bacon, cooked and chopped
- 1 oz package ranch dressing mix
- ½ tbsp black pepper
- 3 cups rotisserie chicken
- 32 oz tater tots
- 1 ½ cups cheddar cheese, shredded
- ¼ cup flat-leaf parsley, chopped

**Preparation :**
1.Set the temperature knob of the Hamilton Beach' toaster oven to bake.

2.Rotate the timer knob and let the toaster oven preheat to 350°F. Spray a casserole dish with cooking spray. Set aside.

3.In a mixing bowl, mix cream of chicken soup, sour cream, milk, sauce, lemon juice, bacon, ranch dressing, and black pepper until well mixed.

4.Stir in chicken then transfer the mixture to the casserole dish. Top with tater tots and cheese.

5.Cover the dish and bake for 30 minutes. Uncover and bake for an additional 15 minutes or until golden brown.

6.Serve and enjoy.

Serving suggestions : serve topped with parsley and rosemary

Variation tip : substitute cheddar cheese with your favourite type

**Nutritional value per Serving :** Calories: 786 kcal, Protein: 28g, Fat: 52g, Carbs: 50g

# 55

# TURKEY MUSHROOM TETRAZZINI

**Preparation Time :** 25 minutes
**Cooking Time :** 25 minutes
**Serving :** 6
**Ingredients :**
• 8 oz spaghetti, cooked
• 3 tbsp cornstarch
• 14 ½ oz chicken broth, reduced-sodium
• ½ tbsp seasoned salt
• A dash of pepper
• 1 tbsp butter
• ¼ cup chopped onion, chopped
• 1 garlic clove, minced
• 12 oz evaporated milk, fat free
• 2 ½ cups turkey breast
• 4 oz mushrooms, drained
• 2 tbsp parmesan cheese
• ¼ tbsp paprika
**Preparation :**
1.Set the temperature knob of the Hamilton Beach' toaster oven to bake.

2.Rotate the timer knob and let the toaster oven preheat to 350°F.

3.Mix cornstarch, broth, and seasoning until well mixed.

4.In a saucepan over medium heat, sauté onions until tender. Add garlic and cook for 1 minute.

5.Add cornstarch mixture to the saucepan and bring to boil. Stir for 2 minutes or until thickened.

6.Reduce heat to low and add milk. Cook and stir for 3 minutes, then stir in turkey, mushrooms, and spaghetti.

7.Transfer everything to a greased baking dish. Bake while covered for 20 minutes.

8.Sprinkle with cheese and paprika. Bake, while uncovered for 10 minutes or until the cheese, has melted.

Serving suggestions : serve with your favourite salad or some raw veggies

Variation tip : you may add sage, mushrooms, and carrots for more flavour and adding veggies to the dish

**Nutritional value per Serving :** Calories: 331 kcal, Protein: 28g, Fat: 5g, Carbs: 41g

# 56

# CHICKEN CORDON BLEU BAKE

Preparation Time :20 minutes

Cooking Time :40 minutes

**Serving :**6

**Ingredients :**

•10 ¾ oz cream of chicken soup, condensed

•1 cup milk

•8 cups cooked chicken, cubed

•½ tbsp pepper

•¾ lb deli ham, cut into strips

•1 cup Swiss cheese, shredded

•3 cups cheddar cheese, shredded

•12 oz stuffing mix, reduced-sodium

**Preparation :**

1.Set the temperature knob of the Hamilton Beach' toaster oven to bake.

2.Rotate the timer knob and let the toaster oven preheat to 350°F.

3.Meanwhile, mix cream of soup with milk in a mixing bowl.

4.Toss chicken with pepper and divide between 2 greased baking dishes.

5.Layer with deli ham, Swiss cheese, 1 cup cheddar, cream of soup mixture, and stuffing. Sprinkle with the remaining cheddar cheese.

6.Bake while covered for 30 minutes, uncover and bake for additional 10 minutes.

7.Let rest for some minutes before serving.

Serving suggestions : serve with Dijon mustard and garlic butter rice

Variation tip : you may use sharp cheddar in place of regular cheddar since it has aged and is rich in flavours.

**Nutritional value per Serving :** Calories: 555 kcal, Protein: 46g, Fat: 29g, Carbs: 26g

## 57

# CHICKEN CLUB CASSEROLES

**Preparation Time :** 20 minutes
**Cooking Time :** 35 minutes
**Serving :** 10
**Ingredients :**
•4 cups spiral pasta, uncooked
•4 cups cooked chicken, cubed
•75 oz condensed cheddar cheese soup
•1 cup cooked bacon, crumbled
•1 cup 2% milk
•1 cup mayonnaise
•4 tomatoes, chopped
•3 cups fresh baby spinach
•2 cups Colby-Monterey Jack cheese
**Preparation :**
1.Cook the spiral pasta according to package directions.
2.Set the temperature knob of the Hamilton Beach' toaster oven to bake setting.
3.Rotate the timer knob to light and allow the toaster oven to preheat to 375° F.

4.Meanwhile mix the chicken, soup, bacon, milk, and mayonnaise in a bowl.

5.Stir in tomatoes and spinach to the chicken mixture.

6.Drain the pasta and stir it into the chicken mixture.

7.Transfer the chicken mixture into 2 casserole dishes then sprinkle with cheese. Cover the casserole dishes.

8.Set the timer to bake the chicken for 35 minutes.

9.Serve and enjoy.

Serving suggestions : serve these chicken casseroles with mashed potatoes.

Variation tip : tomatoes can be replaced with green pepper.

**Nutritional value per Serving :** Calories: 548 kcal, Protein: 33g, Fat: 34g, Carbs: 36g

## 58

# GOLDEN CHICKEN CORDON BLEU

**Preparation Time :** 20 minutes
**Cooking Time :** 20 minutes
**Serving :** 2
**Ingredients :**
•2 chicken breast halves, boneless and skinless
•2 slices deli ham
•2 slices of Swiss cheese
•½ cup all-purpose flour
•¼ tbsp salt
•⅛ tbsp paprika
•⅛ tbsp pepper
•1 egg
•2 tbsp 2% milk
•½ cup seasoned bread crumbs
•1 tbsp canola oil
•1 tbsp melted butter
•Cooking spray
**Preparation :**
1.Sct the temperature knob of the Hamilton Beach' toaster oven to bake setting.

2.Rotate the timer knob to light and allow the toaster oven to preheat to 350° F.

3.Flatten the chicken and top each half with a slice of ham and cheese.

4.Roll up the chicken and tuck in the ends with toothpicks.

5.In a bowl mix flour, salt, paprika, and pepper.

6.Whisk the egg and milk in another bowl.

7.Put the bread crumbs in a shallow dish.

8.Dip the chicken in the flour mixture, then dip in the egg mixture, and finally coat with the breadcrumbs.

9.Brown the chicken in a skillet in oil.

10. Transfer the chicken to a baking dish that has been greased with cooking spray.

11. Bake the chicken for 20 minutes.

12. Transfer the chicken to a serving platter and discard the toothpicks.

13. Drizzle the chicken with butter and serve.

Serving suggestions : serve this chicken with chicken broth gravy.

Variation tip : Swiss cheese can be replaced with Monterey Jack cheese.

**Nutritional value per Serving :** Calories: 501 kcal, Protein: 49g, Fat: 23g, Carbs: 23g

# 59

# TURKEY MEATLOAF

**Preparation Time :** 15 minutes

**Cooking Time :** 1 hour

**Serving :** 10

**Ingredients :**

• 1 cup quick-cooking oats

• 1 chopped onion

• $\frac{1}{2}$ cup carrot, shredded

• $\frac{1}{2}$ cup fat-free milk

• $\frac{1}{4}$ cup egg substitute

• 2 tbsp ketchup

• 1 tbsp garlic powder

• $\frac{1}{4}$ tbsp pepper

• 2 lb lean ground turkey

• Cooking spray

**Preparation :**

1.Set the temperature knob of the Hamilton Beach' toaster oven to bake setting.

2.Rotate the timer knob to light and allow the toaster oven to preheat to 350° F.

3.Meanwhile, in a bowl mix all the ingredients except the turkey until well combined.

4.Add the turkey to the bowl and mix well.

5.Transfer the turkey mixture to a loaf pan coated with cooking spray

6.Mix the topping ingredients and spread over the loaf.

Set the timer to bake the meatloaf for 1 hour.

7. Allow the loaf to cool for 10 minutes before slicing.

8. Serve and enjoy

Serving suggestions : serve this meatloaf with creamed peas.

Variation tip : quick-cooking oats can be replaced with breadcrumbs.

**Nutritional value per Serving :** Calories: 195 kcal, Protein: 20g, Fat: 8g, Carbs: 12g

# 60

# CHICKEN REUBEN ROLL-UPS

**Preparation Time :** 10 minutes

**Cooking Time :** 20 minutes

**Serving :** 2

**Ingredients :**

•2 slices swirled rye and pumpernickel bread

•2 chicken breast halves, boneless and skinless

•$\frac{1}{4}$ tbsp garlic salt

•$\frac{1}{4}$ tbsp pepper

•2 slices of Swiss cheese

•2 slices deli corned beef

•2 tbsp thousand island salad dressing

**Preparation :**

1.Set the temperature knob of the Hamilton Beach' toaster oven to bake setting.

2.Rotate the timer knob to light and allow the toaster oven to preheat to 425° F.

3.Tear the bread into small pieces and pulse them in a blender to form coarse bread crumbs.

4.Flatten the chicken into $\frac{1}{4}$ inch thickness.

5.Sprinkle the chicken with garlic salt and pepper then top with cheese and corned beef.

6.Roll the chicken and tuck in the ends with toothpicks.

7.Brush the chicken rolls with the dressing and coat them with breadcrumbs.

8.Place the rolls on a baking sheet that has been oiled with cooking spray with the seam side down.

9.Bake the rolls for 20 minutes.

10. Transfer the chicken rolls to a serving platter.

11. Serve and enjoy

Serving suggestions : serve these chicken rolls with salad.

Variation tip : corned beef can be replaced with turkey pastrami.

**Nutritional value per Serving :** Calories: 326 kcal, Protein: 32g, Fat: 13g, Carbs: 18g

# FISH AND SEAFOOD
# RECIPES

# 61

# SHRIMP WITH GARLIC BUTTER

**Preparation Time :** 10 minutes

**Cooking Time :** 6 minutes

**Serving :** 1

**Ingredients :**

•1 garlic clove, minced

•$\frac{1}{2}$ small shallot

•$\frac{1}{2}$ tbsp parsley, chopped

•2 tbsp butter, soft

•6 shrimps, peeled and deveined

•Salt

•Ground pepper

**Preparation :**

1.Set the temperature knob of the Hamilton Beach' toaster oven to broil setting and line the tray with foil.

2.In a mixing bowl, mix garlic, shallot, parsley, and butter.

3.Season the shrimp with salt and pepper then brush with the garlic butter mixture.

4.Place the shrimp on the lined tray. Broil at 425°F for 5 minutes or until the shrimp turns opaque.

5.Serve and enjoy.

Serving suggestions : serve with a squeeze of lemon and asparagus

Variation tip : you can use olive oil in place of the butter

**Nutritional value per Serving :** Calories: 212 kcal, Protein: 24g, Fat: 126g, Carbs: 3g

# 62

# HAMILTON BEACH' TOASTER OVEN SALMON

**Preparation Time :** 20 minutes
**Cooking Time :** 15 minutes
**Serving :** 4
**Ingredients :**
- 1 ¼ lb salmon fillet, cut into pieces
- 2 tbsp white wine
- 2 tbsp pesto, thawed
- 2 tbsp toasted pine nuts
- 1 lemon halved

**Preparation :**
1.Cover a baking pan with foil then coat the foil with cooking spray. Place salmon fillets on the lined pan with the skin side down.

2.Squeeze lemon over the salmon, and then drizzle with wine. Let marinate for 15 minutes.

3.Meanwhile, set the temperature knob of the Hamilton Beach' toaster oven to broil setting.

4.Rotate the timer knob and let the toaster oven preheat.

5.Spread ½ tbsp of pesto over each serving of salmon.

6.Broil at 425°F for 5 minutes or until the salmon is opaque.

7.Garnish with pine nuts then squeeze the remaining half lemon.

Serving suggestions : serve with a sauce of your choice and more lemon squeeze.

Variation tip : use non-alcoholic beer in place of white wine

**Nutritional value per Serving :** Calories: 326 kcal, Protein: 39g, Fat: 17g, Carbs: 2g

# 63

## HAMILTON BEACH' TOASTER OVEN BAKED SOLE WITH ASPARAGUS

Preparation Time :10 minutes

Cooking Time :16 minutes

**Serving :**2

**Ingredients :**

Cooking spray

•½ lb uncooked asparagus, trimmed

•1 tbsp olive oil

•½ tbsp salt

•¼ tbsp black pepper

•3 tbsp parmesan cheese, grated

•2 tbsp panko breadcrumbs

•2 tbsp reduced-calorie mayonnaise

•1 tbsp chives, minced

•8 oz uncooked sole

•¼ lemon, cut into 2 wedges

**Preparation :**

1.Set the temperature knob of the Hamilton Beach' toaster oven to bake setting.

2.Rotate the timer knob and let the toaster oven preheat to 450°F

3.Coat a shallow baking dish with cooking spray.

4.Place asparagus in half of the dish then drizzle with oil. Season with salt and pepper.

5.Combine cheese and breadcrumbs on a plate. Season with salt and pepper.

6.In a mixing bowl, mix mayonnaise and chives.

7.Brush one side of the fillet with the mayo mixture, then press that side into the cheese mixture. Place the fish coated side up on the other half of the dish.

8.Place the dish in the toaster oven and bake for 16 minutes or until cooked through.

Serving suggestions : serve with lemon wedges and squeeze more lemon on the fillet

Variation tip : use parmigianno reggiano cheese instead of parmesan

**Nutritional value per Serving :** Calories: 490 kcal, Protein: 33g, Fat: 36g, Carbs: 11g

## 64

# GARLIC BUTTER ORANGE ROUGHLY

**Preparation Time :** 10 minutes
**Cooking Time :** 25 minutes
**Serving :** 4
**Ingredients :**
•½ lb orange roughly, cut into fillets
•2 tbsp butter
•3 garlic cloves, minced
•1 tbsp olive oil
•Salt and pepper
**Preparation :**
1.Set the temperature knob of the Hamilton Beach' toaster oven to bake setting.
2.Rotate the timer knob and let the toaster oven preheat to 375°F.
3.Wash, rinse, and pat dry the fillets with a paper towel. Set aside.
4.Melt butter in a saucepan. Add garlic cloves and oil. Stir until well mixed.
5.Grease a baking dish with oil or cooking spray. Sprinkle

both sides of the fish with salt and pepper, then lay them on a baking dish.

6.Pour garlic mixture over everything and bake for 20 minutes or until the fillets flake.

7.Serve and enjoy.

Serving suggestions : serve with Roasted potatoes, cherry tomatoes, and green beans.

Variation tip : you can add paprika, capers, and cheese when the fish is almost cooked through

**Nutritional value per Serving :** Calories: 263 kcal, Protein: 19g, Fat: 18g, Carbs: 4g

# 65

# SALMON AND ASPARAGUS

**Preparation Time :** 10 minutes
**Cooking Time :** 25 minutes
**Serving :** 4
**Ingredients :**
•Cooking spray
•12 spears of uncooked asparagus, trimmed
•1 tbsp olive oil
•1 tbsp salt
•6 oz uncooked salmon
**Preparation :**
1.Set the temperature knob of the Hamilton Beach' toaster oven to bake setting.
2.Rotate the timer knob and let the toaster oven preheat to 450°F
3.Coat a round baking dish with cooking spray.
4.Place asparagus on half of the baking dish. Sprinkle with oil and season with salt and pepper. Place salmon on the other half of the baking dish.
5.Bake for 16 minutes or until asparagus is tender and the fish is well cooked.

6.Serve and enjoy.

Serving suggestions : squeeze lemon juice on each plate and add a tbsp of Dijon mustard.

Variation tip : you can substitute olive oil with butter or ghee.

**Nutritional value per Serving :** Calories: 246 kcal, Protein:141, Fat: 6g, Carbs: 2g

# 66

# HAMILTON BEACH' TOASTER OVEN SALT GRILLED MACKEREL

**Preparation Time :** 5 minutes

**Cooking Time :** 20 minutes

**Serving :** 4

**Ingredients :**

•4 mackerel fillet

•2 tbsp sake

•1 tbsp salt

•Lemon wedges

**Preparation :**

1.Coat the fish with sake and pat dry with a paper towel.

2.Sprinkle with salt on both sides and let rest for 20 minutes. Wipe any excess moisture expelled from the fish.

3.Set the temperature knob of the Hamilton Beach' toaster oven to bake setting.

4.Rotate the timer knob and let the toaster oven preheat to 400°F

5.Place the fish on a lined baking sheet skin side down. Bake for 15 minutes or until the fish is fully cooked.

6.Flip the fish and transfer the baking pan to the top position. Cook for an additional 5 minutes. Serve when hot.

Serving suggestions : serve with a squeeze of lemon and some sautéed veggies

Variation tip :

**Nutritional value per Serving :** Calories: 278 kcal, Protein: 23g, Fat: 20g, Carbs: 0g

# 67

# WALNUT AND OAT-CRUSTED SALMON

**Preparation Time :** 15 minutes
**Cooking Time :** 15 minutes
**Serving :** 2
**Ingredients :**
•2 salmon fillets, skin removed
•¼ tbsp salt
•¼ tbsp pepper
•3 tbsp quick-cooking oats
•3 tbsp California walnuts, finely chopped
•2 tbsp olive oil
**Preparation :**
1.Set the temperature knob of the Hamilton Beach' toaster oven to bake setting.
2.Rotate the timer knob to med and allow the toaster oven to preheat to 400° F.
3.Sprinkle the salmon with salt and pepper.
4.In a bowl mix the oats, walnuts, and oil.
5.Coat the salmon with the oats mixture and place it on a baking sheet.
6.Set the timer to bake the salmon for 15 minutes.

7.Transfer the salmon to a serving platter.

8.Serve and enjoy.

Serving suggestions : serve this salmon with lemon wedges.

Variation tip : additional seasonings can be used.

**Nutritional value per Serving :** Calories: 484 kcal, Protein: 32g, Fat: 37g, Carbs: 7g

## 68

# WALNUT-CRUSTED GINGER SALMON

**Preparation Time :** 10 minutes
**Cooking Time :** 25 minutes
**Serving :** 4
**Ingredients :**
- 1 tbsp brown sugar
- 1 tbsp reduced-sodium soy sauce
- 1 tbsp Dijon mustard
- 1 tbsp ground ginger
- ¼ tbsp salt
- 4 salmon fillets
- ⅓ cup walnuts, chopped
- Cooking spray

**Preparation :**
1.Set the temperature knob of the Hamilton Beach' toaster oven to bake setting.

2.Rotate the timer knob to med and allow the toaster oven to preheat to 425° F.

3.In a bowl mix sugar, soy sauce, mustard, ginger, and salt until they are well combined.

4.Coat the salmon with the seasoning mixture then sprinkle with walnuts.

5.Place the salmon on a baking pan that has been greased with cooking spray.

6.Set the timer to bake the salmon for 15 minutes.

7.Transfer the salmon to a serving platter.

8.Serve and enjoy.

Serving suggestions : serve these salmon with sautéed greens.

Variation tip : ground ginger can be replaced with fresh ginger.

**Nutritional value per Serving :** Calories: 349 kcal, Protein: 31g, Fat: 22g, Carbs: 6g

# 69

# HAMILTON BEACH' TOASTER OVEN BAKED SHRIMP

**Preparation Time :** 5 minutes
    **Cooking Time :** 2 minutes
    **Serving :** 6
    **Ingredients :**
    •1 lb shrimp
    •1 tbsp avocado oil
    •Kosher salt to taste
    •Freshly ground pepper to taste
    **Preparation :**
    1.Set the temperature knob of the Hamilton Beach' toaster oven to broil setting.
    2.Rotate the timer knob to med and allow the toaster oven to preheat for 5 minutes at 400° F.
    3.Meanwhile, dry the shrimp with a paper towel and put them in a bowl.
    4.Add oil to the shrimp and toss to combine.
    5.Transfer the shrimp to a baking sheet and season them with salt and pepper.
    6.Set the timer to broil the shrimp for 2 minutes.
    7.Transfer the shrimp to a serving platter.

8.Serve and enjoy.

Serving suggestions : Serve the shrimp with chimichurri sauce.

Variation tip : additional seasoning may be used.

**Nutritional value per Serving :** Calories: 85 kcal, Protein: 15g, Fat: 3g, Carbs: 0g

# 70

# CHEESY BAKED SALMON

**Preparation Time :** 10 minutes
**Cooking Time :** 12 minutes
**Serving :** 2
**Ingredients :**
•Two 7 oz salmon fillets
•4 garlic cloves
•Juice from ½ lemon
•Salt to taste
•Ground pepper to taste
•¼ cup mayonnaise
•1 tbsp sugar
•1 tbsp liquid seasoning
•¼ mozzarella cheese, grated
**Preparation :**
1.Set the temperature knob of the Hamilton Beach' toaster oven to bake setting.
2.Rotate the timer knob to med and allow the toaster oven to preheat to 400° F.
3.Rub the salmon with garlic, lemon juice, salt, and pepper.
4.Place the salmon on a baking sheet with the skin side down.

5.In a bowl mix mayonnaise, sugar, and liquid seasoning.

6.Pour the seasoning mixture over the salmon then top with cheese.

7.Bake the salmon for 12 minutes.

8.Transfer the salmon to a serving platter.

9.Serve and enjoy.

Serving suggestions : serve the salmon with lemon wedges.

Variation tip : mozzarella cheese can be replaced with quick-melting cheese.

**Nutritional value per Serving :** Calories: 298 kcal, Protein: 23g, Fat: 17g, Carbs: 12g

# BREAD, BAGEL, AND PIZZA RECIPES

# 71

# HAMILTON BEACH' TOASTER OVEN BANANA BREAD

**Preparation Time :** 10 minutes
**Cooking Time :** 25 minutes
**Serving :** 4
**Ingredients :**
- 1 very ripe banana, mashed
- 1 egg
- 1 tbsp Greek yogurt
- 1 tbsp canola oil
- ¼ tbsp pure vanilla extract
- ½ cup whole wheat flour
- ¼ cup white sugar, granulated
- ¼ tbsp baking soda
- ¼ tbsp ground cinnamon
- ⅛ tbsp sea salt

**Preparation :**

1.Adjust the cooking rack to the bottom position and Set the temperature knob of the Hamilton Beach' toaster oven to bake setting.

2.Rotate the timer knob and let the toaster oven preheat to 350°F

3.Grease the bottom of a mini loaf pan with oil.

4.In a mixing bowl, mix banana, egg, yogurt, oil, and vanilla. Mix in flour, sugar, baking soda, cinnamon, and sea salt until there are no lumps.

5.Pour the batter in the prepared pan and bake for 28 minutes or until a toothpick inserted at the centre comes out clean.

6.Let the bread cool for 10 minutes before serving.

Serving suggestions : serve with a very hot cup of coffee or tea

Variation tip : use any yogurt you may have in hand and can substitute white sugar with brown, coconut, or light brown sugar

**Nutritional value per Serving :** Calories: 125 kcal, Protein: 3g, Fat: 4g, Carbs: 20g

# 72

# HAMILTON BEACH' TOASTER OVEN BAGUETTES

**Preparation Time :** 10 minutes
**Cooking Time :** 25 minutes
**Serving :** 1 loaf
**Ingredients :**
• ³/₄ tbsp quick yeast
• ¹/₂ tbsp Demerara sugar
• ³/₄ cup of warm water
• 1 cup bread flour plus working dough
• ¹/₂ cup whole wheat flour
• ¹/₂ cup oat flour
• 1 ¹/₄ tbsp salt
**Preparation :**
1.Set the temperature knob of the Hamilton Beach' toaster oven to bake setting.

2.Rotate the timer knob and let the toaster oven preheat to 450°F

3.In a mixing bowl, sprinkle yeast and sugar over warm water and let stand for 5 minutes or until foamy.

4.Stir in bread flour until well combined. Stir in salt and whole wheat flour until it forms stiff dough.

5.Knead the dough on a dusted surface until smooth and elastic. Form a ball with the dough.

6.Place the dough in an oiled bowl and coat it with oil. Cover the bowl with a plastic wrap and let rise.

7.Punch down the risen dough and form a slender loaf.

8.Transfer the loaf to a greased baking sheet and let sit for 30 minutes to let rise.

9.Make diagonal slashes on the loaf and brush the top with cool water.

10. Bake for 23 minutes or until golden brown and the loaf sound hollow when tapped.

11. Let cool before serving

Serving suggestions : serve with a sauce and a cup of hot tea

Variation tip : use all-purpose flour in place of the whole wheat flour

**Nutritional value per Serving :** Calories: 231 kcal, Protein: 8g, Fat: 2g, Carbs: 45g

# 73

# PUMPKIN BREAD

**Preparation Time :** 15 minutes
**Cooking Time :** 1 hour 25 minutes
**Serving :** 8
**Ingredients :**
•Cooking spray
• 1 cup all-purpose flour
• $\frac{1}{2}$ tbsp baking soda
• $\frac{1}{4}$ tbsp ground cinnamon
• $\frac{1}{4}$ tbsp ground nutmeg
• $\frac{1}{4}$ tbsp salt
• $\frac{1}{8}$ tbsp ground garlic cloves
• $\frac{1}{8}$ tbsp ground ginger
• 1 cup pumpkin puree
• $\frac{3}{4}$ cup white sugar
• $\frac{1}{4}$ cup vegetable oil
• 1 egg
• $\frac{1}{4}$ cup walnuts, chopped
**Preparation :**
1.Set the temperature knob of the Hamilton Beach' toaster oven to bake setting.

2.Rotate the timer knob and let the toaster oven preheat to 350°F and coat a loaf pan with cooking spray. Also dust it with a dash of flour and tap the excess

3.In a mixing bowl, mix flour, baking soda, cinnamon, nutmeg, salt, garlic clove, and ginger until well combined

4.In a separate bowl, blend the pumpkin puree with sugar oil, and egg. Gradually add the flour mixture and mix until well incorporated.

5.Pour the mixture into the prepared loaf pan and sprinkle walnuts on top.

6.Bake for 1 hour while covered, uncover, and bake for additional 10 minutes. Let rest before serving.

Serving suggestions : Serve with hot tea or coffee

Variation tip : you may use fresh herbs to replace the dried and ground herbs

**Nutritional value per Serving :** Calories: 234 kcal, Protein:3 g, Fat: 10g, Carbs: 34g

# 74

# HAMILTON BEACH' TOASTER OVEN BAGEL CHIPS

**Preparation Time :** 10 minutes
**Cooking Time :** 15 minutes
**Serving :** 3
**Ingredients :**
•1 bagel, unsliced
•1 tbsp olive oil
•Fine sea salt
**Preparation :**
1.Set the temperature knob of the Hamilton Beach' toaster oven to bake setting.

2.Rotate the timer knob and let the toaster oven preheat to 350°F.

3.Slice the bagel using a serrated knife. Stack the slices and cut them in half down the middle.

4.Add the bagel slices to a mixing bowl and drizzle oil and salt. Toss until well combined.

5.Arrange the bagel slices on an ungreased baking sheet in a single layer.

6.Bake for 10 minutes, flip the bagel pieces and bake for an additional 8 minutes.

7.Allow the chips to cool before serving.

Serving suggestions : serve with sauce of your choice

Variation tip : you may add more seasonings such as garlic and vinegar or use garlic salt in place of regular salt.

**Nutritional value per Serving :** Calories: 110 kcal, Protein: 2g, Fat: 5g, Carbs: 13g

# 75

# HAMILTON BEACH' TOASTER OVEN FRUIT PIZZAS

**Preparation Time :** 5 minutes
 **Cooking Time :** 20 minutes
 **Serving :** 12
 **Ingredients :**
 •17 oz sugar cookie dough, cut into slices
 •6 cream cheese, softened
 •1 tbsp powdered sugar
 •1 lime zest
 •¼ almond extract
 •2 mixed sliced fruit ( kiwi, strawberries, and blueberries)
 **Preparation :**
 1.Set the temperature knob of the Hamilton Beach' toaster oven to bake setting.

2.Rotate the timer knob and let the toaster oven preheat to 350°F.

3.Bake the cookies in the toaster oven for 8 minutes. let rest for 10 minutes or until they have cooled completely.

4.In a mixing bowl, beat cream cheese, sugar, lime zest, almond extract with a hand mixer until smooth.

5.Spread cream cheese mixture on the cookies then top with fruit slices. Serve and enjoy.

Serving suggestions : serve with sauce of choice

Variation tip : you can use homemade cookie dough in place of store-bought cookie dough

**Nutritional value per Serving :** Calories: 587 kcal, Protein: 7g, Fat: 33g, Carbs: 69g

# 76

# ENGLISH MUFFIN PIZZA

Preparation Time :10 minutes

Cooking Time :15 minutes

**Serving :**8

**Ingredients :**

•4 whole-wheat English muffins

•½ tbsp olive oil

•¾ cup pizza sauce

•Salt and black pepper to taste

•1 cup mozzarella cheese, shredded

•½ tbsp Italian seasoning

**Preparation :**

1.Set the temperature knob of the Hamilton Beach' toaster oven to bake setting.

2.Rotate the timer knob and let the toaster oven preheat to 400°F and line a baking sheet with foil.

3.Arrange muffin halves on the baking sheet with the cut side up. Drizzle with olive oil and toast in the toaster oven for 4 minutes.

4.Spoon 1 ½ tbsp of pizza sauce on each muffin and spread it evenly. Sprinkle it with salt and pepper to taste.

5.Top with cheese and Italian seasoning. Bake for 10 minutes or until the cheese has melted and the edges have browned.

Serving suggestions : Serve topped with pepperonis, sautéed veggies such as mushrooms and spinach

Variation tip : you may replace mozzarella cheese with provolone, cheddar or any cheese of your choice

**Nutritional value per Serving :** Calories: 107 kcal, Protein: 6g, Fat: 4g, Carbs: 13g

# 77

# PIZZA TOAST

**Preparation Time :** 5 minutes
**Cooking Time :** 15 minutes
**Serving :** 6
**Ingredients :**
•Non -stick cooking spray
•6 slices soft bread
•6 tbsp prepared pizza sauce
•1 ½ cup mozzarella cheese
• 5 oz mini pepperonis
**Preparation :**
1.Set the temperature knob of the Hamilton Beach' toaster oven to toast setting.
2.Rotate the timer knob to light and allow the toaster oven to preheat at 400° F for 5 minutes.
3.Meanwhile, spray a baking sheet with cooking spray.
4.Set the timer to toast the bread slices for 5 minutes.
5.When the timer has gone off, remove the bread slices from the oven.
6.Spread 1 tablespoon of pizza sauce over each bread slice,

sprinkle ¼ cup mozzarella cheese and finally garnish with 16 mini pepperonis.

7.Set the timer to toast the pizza for an additional 10 minutes.

8.Transfer the pizza toast to a serving platter.

9.Serve and enjoy.

Serving suggestions : serve this pizza toast with salad.

Variation tip : mozzarella cheese can be replaced with cheddar cheese.

**Nutritional value per Serving :** Calories: 219 kcal, Protein: 16g, Fat: 11g, Carbs: 12g

# 78

# HAMILTON BEACH' TOASTER OVEN PIZZA BAGELS

**Preparation Time :** 5 minutes
**Cooking Time :** 10 minutes
**Serving :** 4
**Ingredients :**
•Cooking spray
•2 whole-wheat bagels
•¼ cup marinara sauce
•¼ tbsp Italian seasoning
•⅛ tbsp red pepper flakes
•¾ cup low-moisture mozzarella cheese, shredded
•4 thinly sliced mini sweet peppers
•3 tbsp black olive, sliced
•1 tbsp parmesan cheese
**Preparation :**
1.Set the temperature knob of the Hamilton Beach' toaster oven to toast setting.

2.Rotate the timer knob to light and allow the toaster oven to preheat at 375° F for 5 minutes.

3.Oil the cookie sheet with cooking spray.

4.Cut the bagels into halves and place them in the cookie sheet with the inner side facing up.

5.Spread 1 tablespoon of marinara sauce over each half bagel and sprinkle them with Italian seasoning and red pepper flakes.

6.Cover the bagels with 2 tablespoons of cheese and top them with sweet peppers and olive.

7.Layer 1 tablespoon of remaining cheese on the bagel.

8.Set the timer to toast the bagel for 9 minutes.

9.When the timer has gone off, rotate the timer knob to broil setting.

10. Broil the bagel for 3 minutes.

11. Transfer the pizza bagel to a serving platter.

12. Serve and enjoy.

Serving suggestions : serve these bagels with fresh basil.

Variation tip : marinara sauce can be replaced with your favourite pizza sauce.

**Nutritional value per Serving :** Calories: 423 kcal, Protein: 22g, Fat: 16g, Carbs: 48g

---

# 79

# HAMILTON BEACH' TOASTER OVEN SANDWICHES

**Preparation Time :** 5 minutes
**Cooking Time :** 5 minutes
**Serving :** 1
**Ingredients :**
- 1 French bread sandwich roll
- 4 tbsp pizza sauce
- 20 slice turkey pepperoni
- Mozzarella cheese, shredded

**Preparation :**

1. Set the temperature knob of the Hamilton Beach' toaster oven to toast setting.

2. Rotate the timer knob to light and allow the toaster oven to preheat at 350° F for 5 minutes.

3. Meanwhile, slice the sandwich roll and spread 1 tablespoon of pizza sauce on each slice.

4. Top each sandwich slice with 5 pieces of pepperoni and the desired amount of mozzarella cheese.

5. Set the timer to toast the slices for 5 minutes.

6. Assemble the sandwich and place it on a serving platter.

7. Serve and enjoy.

Serving suggestions : serve this sandwich with fried shallot.

Variation tip : pizza sauce can be replaced with spaghetti sauce.

**Nutritional value per Serving :** Calories: 610 kcal, Protein: 90g, Fat: 9g, Carbs: 37g

# 80

# MINI BAGEL PIZZA SNACKS

**Preparation Time :** 5 minutes
**Cooking Time :** 5 minutes
**Serving :** 2
**Ingredients :**
•2 mini bagel
•4 tbsp marinara sauce
•4 Cabot cracker cuts
•12 mini pepperoni, cut into quarters
**Preparation :**
1.Set the temperature knob of the Hamilton Beach' toaster oven to toast setting.

2.Rotate the timer knob to light and allow the toaster oven to preheat at 350° F for 5 minutes.

3.Line the toaster oven pan with foil.

4.Cut the bagel into halves and place it on the foil with the inner side up.

5.Spread 1 tablespoon of marinara sauce on each bagel and top with a cracker nut.

6.Layer 3 pepperoni pieces on the bagel.

7.Set the timer to toast the bagel for 5 minutes.

8.Transfer to a serving platter.

9.Serve and enjoy.

Serving suggestions : serve these bagels with fresh basil.

Variation tip : mini pepperoni can be replaced with turkey pepperoni.

**Nutritional value per Serving :** Calories: 232 kcal, Protein: 14g, Fat: 6g, Carbs: 30g

# VEGAN AND VEGETARIAN RECIPES

# 81

# HAMILTON BEACH' TOASTER OVEN VEGGIE NACHOS

**Preparation Time :** 10 minutes
**Cooking Time :** 5 minutes
**Serving :** 2
**Ingredients :**
•2 serving tortilla chips, restaurant-style
•½cup shredded cheese
•1 cup baby spinach, torn into pieces
•1/2 cup black beans, cooked
•⅓ cup bell peppers, chopped
•1 jalapeno, sliced
•2 tbsp Greek yogurt, plain and non-fat
•½ lime
•Salt and pepper
•⅓ cup of salsa
•1 avocado, seeded and diced
•¼ cup grape tomatoes, sliced
•2 tbsp cilantro, chopped
•1 green onion, sliced
**Preparation :**

1.Set the temperature knob of the Hamilton Beach' toaster oven to bake setting.

2.Rotate the timer knob and let the toaster oven preheat to 400°F.

3.Spread tortilla chips on a rimmed cookie sheet in a single layer. Sprinkle with 3 tbsp cheese.

4.Top the chips with spinach, beans, bell peppers, and jalapeno peppers slices. Sprinkle with the remaining cheese.

5.Bake for 8 minutes or until the cheese has melted.

6.Meanwhile, mix yogurt and lime juice, then season with salt and pepper.

7.Top the nachos with salsa, avocado, tomatoes, cilantro, and onions. Drizzle with yogurt mixture and serve.

Serving suggestions : serve with avocado sauce

Variation tip : use the available type of cheese and top with as many veggies as you can

**Nutritional value per Serving :** Calories: 186 kcal, Protein: 11g, Fat: 5g, Carbs: 25g

# 82

# HAMILTON BEACH' TOASTER OVEN BAKED TOFU

**Preparation Time :** 15 minutes
**Cooking Time :** 15 minutes
**Serving :** 2
**Ingredients :**
• ½ block firm tofu patted dry
• 1 tbsp nutritional yeast
• 1 tbsp oat flour, gluten-free
• 1 tbsp olive oil
• ½ tbsp garlic powder
• ½ tbsp black pepper
• ¼ tbsp sea salt

**Preparation :**

1.Cover the Hamilton Beach' toaster oven baking sheet with foil.

2.Set the temperature knob of the Hamilton Beach' toaster oven to bake setting and rotate the timer knob to allow the toaster oven to preheat to 400°F.

3.Mix nutritional yeast, flour, oil, garlic, black pepper, and salt in a resealable bag. Add tofu and shake until well coated.

4.Place tofu on a baking sheet in a single layer and bake for 30 minutes turning the tofu every 10 minutes.

Serving suggestions : serve over salad, in a stir fry, or stuffed in a sandwiched

Variation tip : you can use twin oak tofu in place of firm tofu

**Nutritional value per Serving :** Calories: 100 kcal, Protein: 8g, Fat: 6g, Carbs: 5g

**83**

# GARLICKY MUSHROOMS

**Preparation Time :** 10 minutes
**Cooking Time :** 12 minutes
**Serving :** 4
**Ingredients :**
•1 lb button mushrooms
•1 tbsp extra virgin olive oil
•2 garlic cloves, minced
•2 tbsp fresh chives, sliced
•⅛ tbsp kosher salt
•⅛ tbsp black pepper
•⅛ tbsp garlic powder
**Preparation :**
1.Set the temperature knob of the Hamilton Beach' toaster oven to bake setting and rotate the timer knob to allow the toaster oven to preheat to 400°F.

2.Meanwhile, place mushrooms in a mixing bowl and add oil, garlic, chives salt, pepper. Toss until well coated.

3.Scatter mushrooms on a baking dish and dust with garlic powder.

4.Bake for 12 minutes. Serve warm.

Serving suggestions : Serve with grilled or baked proteins such as ribeye steaks or pasta

Variation tip : You can add any type of cheese if you like

**Nutritional value per Serving :** Calories: 59 kcal, Protein: 3g, Fat: 3g, Carbs: 4g

# 84

# TOASTER OVEN VEGETABLES

**Preparation Time :** 7 minutes
**Cooking Time :** 50 minutes
**Serving :** 2
**Ingredients :**
- 3 red potatoes, uncooked and quartered
- 1 red onion, cut into wedges
- $\frac{1}{4}$ tbsp salt
- $\frac{1}{8}$ tbsp black pepper
- $\frac{1}{4}$ cups chicken broth, reduced-sodium
- 2 tbsp fresh thyme, chopped
- 2 tbsp olive oil

**Preparation :**

1.Set the temperature knob of the Hamilton Beach' toaster oven to bake setting. Rotate the timer knob to allow the toaster oven to preheat to 400°F.

2.Arrange the potato wedges on a shallow baking pan. Sprinkle with salt and pepper.

3.Pour in chicken broth and sprinkle with thyme.

4.Cover the pan with foil and bake for 20 minutes. Uncover,

flip the potatoes and onions, drizzle with oil then bake for an additional 20 minutes.

Serving suggestions : serve with sauce and garnished with fresh thyme

Variation tip : you can replace red potatoes with fingerlings, or blue potatoes

**Nutritional value per Serving :** Calories: 205 kcal, Protein: 4g, Fat: 14g, Carbs: 19g

# 85

# HAMILTON BEACH' TOASTER OVEN BRUSSELS SPROUTS

**Preparation Time :** 30 minutes
   **Cooking Time :** 25 minutes
   **Serving :** 6
   **Ingredients :**
•2 lb fresh Brussels sprouts
• 1 tbsp olive oil
• $\frac{1}{2}$ tbsp salt
• $\frac{1}{4}$ tbsp pepper
• $\frac{3}{4}$ cup sourdough, cubed
• 1 tbsp butter
• 1 tbsp fresh parsley, minced
• 2 coarsely chopped garlic cloves
• 1 cup heavy whipping cream
• $\frac{1}{8}$ tbsp red pepper flakes, crushed
• $\frac{1}{8}$ tbsp ground nutmeg
• $\frac{1}{2}$ white sharp cheddar cheese, shredded
**Preparation :**
1.Set the temperature knob of the Hamilton Beach' toaster oven to bake setting.

2.Rotate the timer knob to light and allow the toaster oven to preheat to 450° F.

3.Meanwhile, put the Brussels sprouts, ¼ tablespoon, and ⅛ tablespoon pepper and toss to coat.

4.Transfer the Brussels sprouts to a baking pan and bake them for 10 minutes.

5.Rotate the temperature knob to reduce the temperature to 400° F.

6.Pulse the sough dough, butter, parsley, and garlic using a blender to form fine crumbs.

7.Transfer the Brussels to a baking dish.

8.In a bowl, mix the cream, pepper flakes, nutmeg, and the remaining salt and pepper.

9.Pour the cream mixture over the Brussels then sprinkle with cheese.

10. Top the Brussels with the crumbs and bake them uncovered for 15 minutes.

11. Transfer the Brussels to a serving platter. Serve and enjoy.

Serving suggestions : serve these Brussels sprouts with grilled pork chops.

Variation tip : sourdough can be replaced with French bread.

**Nutritional value per Serving :** Calories: 283 kcal, Protein: 8g, Fat: 22g, Carbs: 16g

# 86

# GREEN BEAN CASSEROLE

**Preparation Time :** 15 minutes
**Cooking Time :** 35 minutes
**Serving :** 10
**Ingredients :**
•22 oz condensed cream of mushroom soup, undiluted
•1 cup whole milk
•2 tbsp soy sauce
•$\frac{1}{8}$ tbsp pepper
•32 oz frozen green beans, cooked and drained
•6 oz French fried onions
**Preparation :**
1.Set the temperature knob of the Hamilton Beach' toaster oven to bake setting.
2.Rotate the timer knob to light and allow the toaster oven to preheat at 350° F.
3.In a bowl mix the soup, milk, soy sauce, and pepper.
4.Stir in the beans to the soup mixture.
5.Transfer half of the bean mixture to a baking dish and sprinkle with half of the onions.

6.Top the baking dish with the remaining beans and sprinkle with the remaining onions.

7.Set the timer to bake the beans for 35 minutes.

8.Transfer the beans to a serving platter.

9.Serve and enjoy.

Serving suggestions : serve these beans with rice.

Variation tip : cream of mushroom soup can be replaced with different cream soups.

**Nutritional value per Serving :** Calories: 163 kcal, Protein: 2g, Fat: 11g, Carbs: 14g

# 87

# VEGAN GREEN BEANS CASSEROLE

**Preparation Time :** 20 minutes
**Cooking Time :** 25 minutes
**Serving :** 16
**Ingredients :**
- 2 tbsp olive oil
- 8 oz fresh mushrooms, sliced
- 1 chopped onion
- 3 minced garlic cloves
- 3 cups dairy-free sour cream
- 1 tbsp salt
- ½ tbsp ground black pepper
- 36 oz frozen cut green beans, thawed
- 4 cups dairy-free cheddar-flavoured cheese, shredded
- ¼ cup dairy-free buttery spread
- 1 cup crushed Ritz crackers
- 1 cup french-fried onions, coarsely chopped

**Preparation :**
1.Set the temperature knob of the Hamilton Beach' toaster oven to bake setting.

2.Rotate the timer knob to light and allow the toaster oven to preheat to 350° F.

3.Meanwhile, heat oil in a skillet over medium heat and sauté the mushrooms and onions.

4.Stir in garlic to the skillet and cook for 1 minute.

5.Stir in the sour cream, salt, and pepper to the skillet until well combined.

6.Add the green beans and cheese and mix until they are well coated.

7.Transfer the bean mixture to a baking dish.

8.In another skillet melt the buttery spread.

9.Stir in the crackers and fried onions in the butter.

10. Sprinkle the butter mixture over the casserole.

11. Set the timer knob to bake the casserole for 25 minutes.

12. Transfer the beans to a serving platter.

13. Serve and enjoy.

Serving suggestions : serve these vegan green beans with rice.

Variation tip : Brussel sprouts can be replaced with broccoli.

**Nutritional value per Serving :** Calories: 327 kcal, Protein: 3g, Fat: 23g, Carbs: 26g

# 88

# YOGURT CORNBREAD

**Preparation Time :** 10 minutes
**Cooking Time :** 25 minutes
**Serving :** 9
**Ingredients :**
•1 cup yellow cornmeal
•¼ cup all-purpose flour
•2 tbsp baking powder
•½ tbsp salt
•¼ tbsp baking soda
•1 egg, lightly beaten
•1 cup fat-free plain yogurt
•½ cup fat-free milk
•¼ cup canola oil
•1 tbsp honey
•Cooking spray
**Preparation :**
1.Set the temperature knob of the Hamilton Beach' toaster oven to bake setting.
2.Rotate the timer knob to light and allow the toaster oven to preheat to 425° F.

3.In a bowl mix the cornmeal, flour, baking powder, salt, and baking soda.

4.In another bowl mix the egg, yogurt, milk, oil, and honey.

5.Mix all the ingredients until well mixed.

6.Pour the batter into a baking dish.

7.Set the timer to bake the bread for 20 minutes.

8.Transfer the bread to a serving platter.

9.Serve and enjoy.

Serving suggestions : serve this cornbread with sautéed greens.

Variation tip : cornmeal can be replaced with corn grits.

**Nutritional value per Serving :** Calories: 157 kcal, Protein: 4g, Fat: 7g, Carbs: 20g

# 89

# LENTIL LOAF

**Preparation Time :** 35 minutes
**Cooking Time :** 45 minutes
**Serving :** 6
**Ingredients :**
- ¾ brown lentils
- 15 oz vegetable broth
- Cooking spray
- 1 tbsp olive oil
- 1 ¾ cups carrot, shredded
- 1 cup onion, finely chopped
- 1 cup fresh mushrooms, chopped
- 2 tbsp fresh basil, minced
- 1 tbsp fresh parsley, minced
- 1 cup part-skim mozzarella cheese, shredded
- ½ cup cooked brown rice
- 1 egg
- 1 egg white
- ½ tbsp salt
- ½ tbsp garlic powder
- ¼ tbsp pepper

•2 tbsp tomato paste

•2 tbsp water

**Preparation :**

1.Put the lentils and broth in a saucepan and bring to a boil over medium heat.

2.Allow the lentils to simmer at a reduced heat for 30 minutes.

3.Set the temperature knob of the Hamilton Beach' toaster oven to bake setting.

4.Rotate the timer knob to light and allow the toaster oven to preheat to 350° F.

5.Line a loaf pan with parchment paper and coat it with cooking spray.

6.Heat oil in a skillet over medium heat and sauté carrots, onion, and mushrooms for 10 minutes.

7.Stir in the basil and parsley and transfer the vegetables to a bowl.

8.Stir in the cheese, rice, egg white, salt, garlic powder, pepper, and lentils to the vegetables until well combined.

9.Transfer the lentil loaf to the loaf pan.

10. In a shallow dish, mix the tomato paste and water then spread over the loaf.

11. Set the timer to bake the loaf for 45 minutes.

12. Allow the loaf to cool for 10 minutes before slicing.

13. Serve and enjoy.

Serving suggestions : serve this lentil loaf with vegetarian gravy

Variation tip : rice can be replaced with quick-cooking oats

**Nutritional value per Serving :** Calories: 213 kcal, Protein: 14g, Fat: 5g, Carbs: 29g

# 90

# SCALLOPED POTATOES

**Preparation Time :** 25 minutes

**Cooking Time :** 1 hour

**Serving :** 6

**Ingredients :**

•2 tbsp butter

•3 tbsp all-purpose flour

•1 tbsp salt

•¼ tbsp pepper

•1 ½ cup fat-free milk

•½ cup reduced-fat cheddar cheese, shredded

•2 lb red potatoes, peeled and thinly sliced

•1 cup onions, thinly sliced

**Preparation :**

1.Set the temperature knob of the Hamilton Beach' toaster oven to bake setting.

2.Rotate the timer knob to light and allow the toaster oven to preheat to 350° F.

3.In a saucepan melt butter over medium heat.

4.Stir in flour, salt, and pepper into the butter.

5.Whisk milk gradually into the butter mixture and allow it to cook for 2 minutes ensuring that you stir occasionally.

6.Remove the sauce from heat and stir in cheese until it melts.

7.Grease a baking dish with cooking spray.

8.Put half the potatoes into the dish, and then layer half the onion on the potatoes and finally top with the sauce.

9.Repeat step 8 so that uniform layers are formed.

10. Cover the baking dish and place it in the toaster oven.

11. Set the timer to bake the potatoes for 50 minutes.

12. When the timer has gone off uncover the baking dish and bake for an additional 10 minutes.

13. Transfer the potatoes to a serving platter.

14. Serve and enjoy.

Serving suggestions : serve these potatoes with baked chicken.

Variation tip : fat-free milk can be replaced with 2%milk.

**Nutritional value per Serving :** Calories: 215 kcal, Protein: 8g, Fat: 6g, Carbs: 32g

# CONCLUSION

As you can see from the guide and recipes above, there is more to Hamilton Beach toaster ovens than just appealing to your eyes. They clearly permit you to easily prepare your favourite dishes while saving on time and energy. This is an appliance you must add to your kitchen appliances.

CPSIA information can be obtained
at www.ICGtesting.com
Printed in the USA
BVHW080603260421
605848BV00009B/483